St. Louis Community College

Forest Park
Florissant Valley
Meramec

Instructional Resources
St. Louis, Missouri

GAYLORD

ONE VOICE

....

ONE VOICE

A Pulitzer Prize-winning journalist tells stories about the black experience

TONI Y. JOSEPH

Published by
The Dallas-Fort Worth Association of Black Communicators
400 S. Record St., Lock Box 11, Dallas, Texas 75202

Cover design and page design by Marilyn Glaser
Cover artwork photographed by Jason Miccolo Johnson

(ISBN: 1-56530-139-0)

To Toni's cherished nephew,
Antonio Foushee

Proceeds from the sale of *One Voice*
go toward the establishment
of an endowed college scholarship fund
in the memory of
Toni Y. Joseph.
Money earned from the fund
will be awarded annually
by the
Dallas-Fort Worth Association of Black Communicators
to black journalism students.
For more information
or to make additional contributions, contact:

Toni Y. Joseph Scholarship Fund
Dallas-Fort Worth Association of Black Communicators
400 S. Record St., Lock Box 11
Dallas, Texas 75202

CONTENTS

■■■■■■■■■■

SECTION 1: RAGE & PRIDE

My Life as a Slave: *At a workshop designed to help African Americans break their bonds with the horrors of the past, the writer and others are given the unenviable task of spending the day as slaves.* **3**

Renaissance of Pride: *As the 1990s dawn, a growing number of African Americans embrace anew a philosophy of black consciousness.* **7**

Chronicle of Frustration: *In her book,* Volunteer Slavery, *journalist Jill Nelson writes of the "professional and psychic and emotional devastation" she suffered during her years at* The Washington Post. **12**

A Professor's Passion: *Princeton University philosopher Cornel West weathers the storms that he's stirred with his essays on racial issues.* **17**

SECTION II: HISTORY LESSONS

Freedman's Memories: *A city's excavation of the graves of former slaves stirs descendants to search for details of those long-distant days.*

23
■

Experiment in Pain: *For 40 years, a U.S. Public Health Department study withheld drugs from syphilis patients, eventually allowing them to die from the disease. But a contemporary film maker is determined to keep their memory alive.*

29
■

Radical Changes: *Former Black Panthers trace the ways in which their membership in the militant party led them onto more peaceful paths of service.*

35
■

Cultivating a Dream: *A love for the soil and the rural way of life keeps African-American farmers fighting impossible odds to stay on their land.*

43
■

SECTION III: HIDDEN TREASURES

Hair-Raising Adventures: *It's one woman's daring 'do — getting fake curls woven into her real hair with, of all things, a rug hook.*

53
■

Table for One: *Cassondra Armstrong is a one-woman cafe crew — chef, waitress, shopper, cashier, dishwasher and dreamer ... of a bigger restaurant with her own staff.*

56
■

Calvin Strong and Tall: *A 7-foot-4 doorman is a standout at one of Dallas' trendiest restaurants.*

62
■

Cuttin' Heads: *Getting your hair cut at Sessions Barber and Beauty Shop is just part of the attraction at the longtime neighborhood institution.*

64
■

Pier Group: *A favorite fishing spot attracts a diversity — rich and poor, old and young, black, white and brown — but all share a devotion to awaiting the next bite.*

68
■

A Good Name: *Joe Blow isn't just a figure of speech. He's a church-going father of three who has learned to live with his generic moniker.*

71
■

SECTION IV: BY THE BOOK

Alice in Wonderland: *Author Alice Walker allows a glimpse into her very private world upon the release of her best-selling book* Possessing the Secret of Joy.

77
■

Ode to Black Men: *Amid pervasive media images of African-American men as criminals and ne'er-do-wells, a number of black women poets contribute to an anthology in celebration of black men.*

84
■

Well Versed: *Poet Tim Seibles begins to develop a wide following and modest acclaim with his engaging, approachable work.*

88
■

Out of the Ashes: *The country's oldest black-owned bookstore is one of the victims of Los Angeles' fiery riots, touched off after four white police officers were found not guilty of beating black motorist Rodney King.*

95
■

Black, White and Read All Over: *A white woman discovers black literature and becomes its champion, organizing a literary festival and snagging a superstar: Toni Morrison.*

99
■

SECTION V: AGAINST ALL ODDS

The Sins of the Son: *Betty Johnson tried her best to raise her son Kevin right. Her best wasn't good enough.*

107
■

Robbed: *Joyce Ann Brown wasn't the only one who suffered when prosecutors misled jurors and sent her to prison for a crime she says she didn't commit.*

114
■

Invisible Men: *Has the black community worsened the AIDS epidemic by turning its back on the gay men in its midst?*

122
■

Empty Places: *When Albert Johnson shipped out for the Persian Gulf War in 1991, he left holes in the lives of his family, his friends — and one fragile boy named Mark.*

129
■

SECTION VI: ANCESTRAL VOICES

A Brush With Destiny: *Artist Lois Mailou Jones once had to ask white friends to submit her works to exhibitions under their names. Now, at age 87, she basks in her renown.*

139
■

Sanctuary: *Why did poet James A. Emanuel abandon the United States for Paris? Because, he says, "you're supposed to run away from things that are killing you."*

143
■

500 Americans in Paris: *Scholars, artists, writers and musicians flock to a conference celebrating African-American expatriates in Europe.* 149 ■

What's Shaking: *A collection of African-inspired music for children brings back happy memories for musicians and listeners.* 154 ■

A View From the Left: *"I'm an organizer, not a writer," says Louise Patterson. But finally the woman at the center of the Harlem Renaissance is ready to tell her story.* 157 ■

SECTION VII: THE NEXT GENERATION

In Search of Family: *More than half of the adoptable children in the United States are black — a problem that has concerned adults scrambling for solutions.* 163 ■

Comic Relief: *Assistant district attorney by day, vigilante by night — he's Brotherman, the star of the first comic book targeted at young African-American readers.* 169 ■

When Children Become Violent: *African-American youths may be no more troubled than their white peers, but they are more likely to turn their turmoils outward, wreaking havoc as they wreck their lives.* 173 ■

Rite of Passage: *Four teenagers celebrate their transition from childhood to adulthood with a ceremony rooted in African tradition.* 179 ■

ONE VOICE ▪ TONI Y. JOSEPH

SECTION VIII: A WOMAN'S BURDEN

Women of Decision: *While black women have abortions at a proportionately higher rate than white women, they traditionally have remained silent about the politics of the issue. Their voices, however, are beginning to resound.*

187
▪

A Healthy Choice: *African-American women are breaking down barriers that have relegated them to lives that are shorter and less healthy than their white counterparts.*

194
▪

Her Strong Suit: *An office clerk gets fed up with her boss' leers and suggestive touches, so she takes him to court. The charge: sexual harassment.*

201
▪

SECTION IX: BLOOD SISTERS

Rite or Wrong? *A young woman flees her native Mali to avoid circumcision — a ritual that cost her best friend her life.*

213
▪

Scarred by Tradition: *In this Pulitzer Prize-winning report, female circumcision is placed at the core of women's role in African society — a life of hardship and degradation.*

219
▪

ACKNOWLEDGEMENTS

■ ■ ■ ■ ■ ■ ■ ■ ■ ■

One Voice has been published under the auspices of the Dallas-Fort Worth Association of Black Communicators, a chapter of the National Association of Black Journalists.

Publication would not have been possible without the generous support from the following:

The Dallas Morning News
The Dow Jones Foundation
The Cleveland Plain Dealer
The Miami Herald

Editing, design and publication of the book were overseen by the Toni Y. Joseph Book Committee, all staff members of *The Dallas Morning News*: Nancy Kruh (chairman), Patricia Gaston, Marilyn Glaser, Sharon Grigsby, Ira Hadnot, Don R. Huff, Jean Nash Johnson, Victoria Loe, Ken Parish Perkins and John Yearwood.

Thanks to artist Lois Mailou Jones who contributed the use of her painting "Maiden of Suriname," which appears on the cover.

Acknowledgements also go to the following:

Margaret Eastman, Marion Faggett, Alison Hamilton, Terry Holt,

Ronnie Lee, Ronald Raburn, David Stjernholm, Lawrence Young, *The Dallas Morning News*; Anjetta McQueen, *The Cleveland Plain Dealer*; Donna Britt, Kevin Merida, *The Washington Post*; Tom Petzinger, *The Wall Street Journal*; Martha Quillin, *The Raleigh, N.C., News & Observer*; Linda Villarosa, *Essence*; Tsitsi Wakhisi, University of Miami; Tritobia H. Benjamin, Howard University; Nancy Matthews, Meridian International Center, Washington, D.C.; Arnold Rampersad, Princeton University; Emma Rodgers, Ashira Tosihwe, Black Images Book Bazaar, Dallas; Karen Ashmore, the Dallas Rainbow Chapter of the National Organization for Women.

Also appreciated is the support and encouragement from Toni Y. Joseph's family: mother, Linda Joseph Caldwell; father, Leslie Joseph; sisters Tanya and Tamika Joseph; and nephew, Antonio Foushee.

SECTION I

·

RAGE
& PRIDE

···········

My Life
As A Slave
■ ■ ■ ■ ■ ■ ■ ■ ■ ■

et busy, nigger," I was told. "This here is one lazy niggress."

Few things make me as mad as the N-word. I never say it, and I challenge other African Americans who do. But I was powerless to stop my tormentor, and I seethed under the weight of my impotence. Whenever I took a step — even a short step — shackles tugged at my ankles, a humiliating reminder that I was the property of the Johnson plantation. Some of the other slaves had begun to daydream, trying to blot out this intolerable reality. All I could do was wonder what I had done to deserve my fate.

Yes, I had asked to join this workshop, designed to help African Americans break the psychological bonds of slavery. But I never expected to spend the day as a slave.

Dr. Na'im Akbar, a Florida State University research scientist, designed the daylong workshop, a first for Dallas and one of the first in the nation. The event drew 100 people from Texas, Tennessee, Arkansas and Louisiana who paid $150 each.

Dr. Akbar and other African-American psychologists and sociologists have long argued that traits developed in response to slavery — misdirected anger, dependence on whites, lack of a clear identity, difficulties in carrying projects to completion — have been passed down from generation to generation.

Anyone skeptical of the theory need only examine the research that shows how the coping mechanisms developed by children of alcoholics later work against them, says Dallas clinical psychologist Brenda Wall, an African American. "The evidence shows that the very survival patterns that allowed us to make it through slavery exist today," Dr. Wall says. "They were counterproductive then, and they're counterproductive today." Hoping to reverse the downward spiral that has trapped much of black America, mental health professionals such as Dr. Akbar are beginning to take their research out of academia, out of private practice and into the streets.

Only African Americans participated in Dr. Akbar's workshop, but those designated as masters showed no mercy to their slaves. Master and slave alike slipped easily into their roles.

The masters told us to keep our heads bowed and speak when spoken to. Slaves who ignored orders were severely beaten. Those who tried to escape were hanged or mutilated. The punishments were symbolic, of course, but the emotions they evoked were devastating nonetheless. Ashira Tosihwe, a master on the Jones plantation, chopped off the hand of a runaway who attempted to incite others to run away.

The masters told us to keep our heads bowed and speak when spoken to. Slaves who ignored orders were severely beaten.

■ ■ ■ ■ ■ ■ ■ ■ ■ ■

"It was too real," says Ms. Tosihwe, co-owner of Black Images Book Bazaar in Dallas. "I felt terrible about the whole thing, but anyone in that role will be evil."

I watched from the corner of my eye while one of my fellow slaves was choked and slapped by a group of overseers after she tried to stab the master with a pair of scissors. My mind filled with every conceivable thought to push out the sounds of snapping whips and screaming slaves.

I thought about my cousins, so keen in their sense of the injustices meted out to blacks, but rarely willing to publicly question authority figures. I thought about the African-American teenagers and adults I encounter while volunteering in the community. They speak candidly to me, but rarely do they look at or talk to Anglo volunteers.

We slaves moved when told to and were forced to work on command. Our task was to cut out pictures and emblems, then use them to decorate a box. Physically restrained, I found that an uncustomary caution had replaced my usual vigor. I watched more than I worked. The only way to assert my independence was to sly-ly produce as little as possible. "This here is one lazy niggress." The words echoed through my brain.

Unfortunately, the workshop wasn't the first time I'd heard the word "lazy" used to describe my people. Certainly, the bulging wel-fare rolls indicate that many can't, or won't, free themselves from dependence.

But the African Americans I've known have always worked hard. By typical American (read: Anglo) standards, most them are also exceptionally well-educated. Harvard, Yale, Stanford, Colum-bia, MIT, University of Chicago, University of Pennsylvania.

Recently, however, my friends have been abandoning success-ful careers like there's no tomorrow. One friend quit "good" jobs as a banker and a journalist, then took off to East Africa on a fre-quent-flyer ticket — with no cash and several credit cards. Usual-ly, when things like that happen I get all worked up, angry at what looks to me like fatalism.

But about halfway through the workshop, I understood a lot better. That was the point at which I was ready to just get up and walk away from my job — and from the masters who were enjoy-ing all the benefits of my labor.

Like our enslaved ancestors, contemporary African Americans are expected to be passive, says Dallas psychotherapist Dr. Linda Webb-Watson, a slave master during the workshop.

"(We) have been trained to work for (Anglos)," she says, "not educated to work for (our)selves."

A female overseer monitored slaves on the Johnson plantation. To demonstrate her authority, she yelled a lot. She invaded our space by planting her body three, maybe four inches away. She held her head so close to ours, we could smell the orange juice that lingered on her lips. We also felt the spit that showered our faces as she opened her mouth to shout.

Hoping to avoid confrontation, I kept my eyes on my sneakers. "What's your name, nigger?" she demanded of another slave. "What's your name?"

She was talking to me. Startled, I mumbled, "Joseph."

"That ain't your name, nigger," she said. "Your name is Johnson. What's your name, nigger?"

By this time, I could feel the blood swirling inside my head. My heart began to palpitate in what felt like a hollow chest. I'd felt this way before. The feeling was fear. The kind of fear that rises in your throat when you know you have no way to escape.

"Johnson," I whispered. "My name is Johnson."

That momentary confrontation illuminated an identity crisis I've grappled with for years. Until Dr. Akbar's workshop, I had managed to suppress the longtime urge to select an African name, cutting my ties to my slave-owner ancestors. On the other hand, I'd privately snickered at African-American women who adopted strange-sounding polysyllabic names for their children.

I also love introducing myself to Anglos whose last name is Joseph. Because the gesture makes them uncomfortable, I immediately tell them that we're probably related — albeit back on the plantation.

By lunchtime, I didn't think I could tolerate another minute of bound feet and silence. I wanted to speak to other slaves. Dr. Akbar instructed the masters to go through the buffet line first, the abolitionists second and the slaves last. I stood with my friend Yvonne and a man whose name is Origin Al.

Mr. Al, who didn't know I was a reporter, ranted about how the media portray African Americans and other minorities. Yvonne, shaken by the whole experience, kept saying, "This is deep."

My thoughts, focused on lunch, revealed how quickly I'd become conditioned to my place.

"You know what they're going to do," I said. "They're going to give real food to everybody else. We're going to get oatmeal or something." Much to my surprise, we got rice and grilled chicken like everyone else. I was grateful for that — but not nearly as grateful as I was for the lessons I learned that day.

May 5, 1990

Renaissance
of Pride

■ ■ ■ ■ ■ ■ ■ ■ ■ ■

This is the year that Darryl Thomas shed his business suits and swaddled his body in dashikis, covered his head with crown hats and slipped his feet into soft leather sandals. This is the year the former Revlon executive stopped selling hair-care products and started peddling black pride from a fragrant boutique in Dallas. The words on the T-shirts that Mr. Thomas sells at his Sandaga Market embody his choice: Black by Popular Demand, Black by Nature, Proud by Choice, By Any Means Necessary, Nat is Back and United We Stand.

"When I wake up in the morning and put on a West African outfit," says Mr. Thomas, "I feel four to five inches taller."

Mr. Thomas' African-rooted perspectives on dress, business and language all reflect a renewed philosophy of black consciousness being increasingly embraced by African Americans young and old, rich and poor. For the fifth time since Africans were brought to the Americas as slaves, a decade is closing with an enthusiastic celebration of black culture and history. The movement is evident in the clothes, arts and scholarship that black people are choosing to express their vision.

'When I wake up in the morning and put on a West African outfit, I feel four to five inches taller.'

■ ■ ■ ■ ■ ■ ■ ■ ■ ■

Experts in black culture believe this renaissance may be rooted in the recent realization that changes in racial attitudes have not permeated the whole of American culture.

For example, incidents of community and campus racism have

alarmed African Americans, says Dr. Lovett Emmack, a political scientist and administrator at California State University at Hayward. Dr. Emmack, who attended the recent Third Eye Black Awakening Conference in Dallas, says that his community feels betrayed, disappointed and angry that anti-discrimination laws were not as sweeping in their effect on society as African Americans hoped they would be.

"Our security is uneasy," Dr. Emmack says. "People are still very afraid they will lose whatever it is they have achieved. Talk to a black who is an officer in a corporation, or talk to a black anywhere." The Rev. Zan Holmes, pastor of St. Luke's Community United Methodist Church, links the devastating rise in crime, teen-age pregnancy, illiteracy and drug abuse to the decrease in social services. He says such problems also demonstrate that increased opportunities have not been widely available.

"We thought we were making progress, and instead we were being lulled into a deep sleep," Mr. Holmes says. "Schools are still segregated, there are widening income gaps and unemployment in our community is still high. I told my people last Sunday, 'Zsa Zsa Gabor cursed a policeman, then slapped him. Suppose she had been one of us? No matter if we had had the biggest job in IBM, no black person in this country — no black person has enough power to get away with that.' It's sobering."

Dallas residents and African Americans across the nation are greeting the situation with a look inward. Lessons from the past and a positive sense of achievement are guiding the community as its future is shaped by a strong sense of self-preservation. They are urgently examining black culture and sharing it with society.

In Dallas, community organizations have moved beyond the calendar limitations of Black History Month to sponsor a number of tributes and conferences throughout the year.

"If you'd told me 10 years ago we'd have these activities in Dallas, I would have laughed in your face," says Cornelius Owens, a member of a black literature study group. "People are using the past as a model to help us determine how we can build for our future."

His reading about black culture — for example, learning that early North Africans developed complex engineering methods and used advanced mathematics — bolstered Mr. Owens' confidence when he accepted a technical position with Delta Air Lines several years ago.

"I was taught in school that the Greeks were the fathers of mathematics and philosophy," Mr. Owens says. "It wasn't until later that I read that Greeks got their information from Africans."

African Americans say it is imperative that they share this type of information with their children to instill pride. North Dallas and suburban parents, concerned that their daughters were isolated from black culture in their schools and neighborhoods, decided this year to guide their teenagers through an African-inspired rite of passage. Cloaked in African costumes, the group will pass into womanhood in a formal program at St. Luke's Community United Methodist Church during Kwanzaa festivities in December.

In one ceremony, participants replace given English names with chosen African names.

Other activities abound. The South Dallas Cultural Center helped sponsor a ceremony in which participants replaced their given English names with chosen African names before a large audience of family and friends. Plans are under way to repeat the program.

Memberships of local reading and study groups that focus on African-American literature have swelled. The monthly meetings of Midnight Birds, a women's literature group that began with 10 members nine years ago, now draw between 50 and 100 participants of both sexes. And last summer, two local historians led 16 children, ages 9 through 13, in a two-week, all-day black history day camp at Lincoln High School.

The black consciousness surge has seeped into area economics, too. Businesses that specialize in Afrocentric products are growing in Dallas' black communities. Sandaga Market, for example, began selling talking drums and other African instruments, fabric, hand-tailored African clothes, message T-shirts, hats and accessories this year.

Fine arts also have captured the imaginations of black consumers. During 1989, four black-owned galleries opened in Dallas, joining at least one other thriving visual arts enterprise. Programs that display black art in the homes of television characters have stimulated a widespread interest.

"We have more exposure now," says Frank Frazier, a nationally known local artist. "I have to admit that Bill Cosby has been a big help."

'We have more exposure now. I have to admit that Bill Cosby has been a big help.'

■ ■ ■ ■ ■ ■ ■ ■ ■ ■

Ebony Fine Arts Gallery and Ann Taylor Gallery offer affordable prints, posters, gifts and a few original pieces, while Roots sells original paintings by local artists. Visions in Black features Mr. Frazier's work and deals in original pieces by nationally acclaimed African-American artists such as Romare Beardon and Jacob Lawrence.

Black literature, not printed in mass quantities and once hard to find locally, is available. Dallas residents hunting for a volume of poetry by Countee Cullen or some early prose by Langston Hughes can usually find it at Black Images Book Bazaar. The store's vast selection is complemented by volumes available at Pan-African Connection, a bookstore specializing in political literature.

Newspapers in New York, Los Angeles, Washington and other cities report that African Americans are buying out bookstores' stock of black literature and taped speeches by the Rev. Jesse Jackson, minister Louis Farrakhan and the late Rev. Martin Luther King Jr. The tastes of Dallas residents are no different, says Emma Rodgers, Black Images' co-owner.

The figure most sought-after among black youth is Malcolm X. A quotation from the slain Muslim leader exhorting blacks to counter violent attacks with violence is paired with a non-violent missive from Dr. King at the end of Spike Lee's film *Do The Right Thing*. Many also attribute Malcolm X's heightened stature to rap music artists who have replaced an early ethos of self-centered brag-

gadocio with lyrics that expound the nationalism and self-determination the leader so passionately preached.

The surge of black pride also manifests itself in apparel. Traditional African clothing and accessories, popular during the 1960s,
now appear in closets all over Dallas. Karen Keaton, a Richardson
day-care center operator, wears loose-fitting, printed pant sets as
she watches her small charges. Her clothing, jewelry and artifacts
provide visual aids for geography, history and culture lessons about
Africa. Even African Americans who work for firms in which busi-
ness-type attire is standard slip on favorite African jewelry or wear
neckties and scarves woven from brightly colored cloth. Leather
pendants bearing an embossed image of Africa are a de rigueur ac-
cessory for students. Close-fitting knit caps, crown hats and cloth
hair wraps adorn the heads of grandfathers and toddlers alike.

Although the clothing may only cover the skin, it is a symbol for
a movement that is more than skin deep, says Dr. W. Marvin Dulaney, assistant professor of history at the University of Texas at Arlington. "Those of us who came out of the '60s did not work hard
enough to unify the community," Dr. Dulaney says. "We're leaving
the '80s having to do many of the same things. Things I thought
everyone had learned — well, they hadn't. The stakes are too high
now. We have no choice. I think some serious education is going
on."

November 20, 1989

Chronicle
of Frustration

▪▪▪▪▪▪▪▪▪▪

Jill Nelson's family wrapped her in love and treated her with respect but forgot to teach her that most other people she would encounter would not do the same.

She learned that lesson when she took a job at *The Washington Post* in 1986. Ms. Nelson expected a place where she would be encouraged to produce good stories, the kind of meaty, sensitive work that for years had earned her kudos as a free-lance magazine writer.

She found, as she describes in her new book, an institution she believed was more interested in her middle-class pedigree, her professional parents, her Ivy League degree and her vacation house on Martha's Vineyard than in the ideas she put forth.

She asserts that *The Post* was more interested in her silent presence as a symbol of integration than in her actual contributions.

"I lived a really charmed life," Ms. Nelson says. "My parents, to their credit, never thought it necessary to prepare me to deal with such negativity. They never had reason to believe I'd be part of it."

By "negativity," Ms. Nelson, 41, means the "professional and psychic and emotional devastation" she says she experienced for four years at the hands of *Washington Post* executives and editors. The resulting memoir, *Volunteer Slavery: My Authentic Negro Experience* (Noble Press), names names and has tongues wagging from Washington, D.C., to Walla Walla, Wash.

"The book is much harder on myself and my family than anyone else," says Ms. Nelson, who writes about her parents' divorce, the chemical addictions of various siblings, her own failed relationships and her struggle for self-acceptance.

"I don't think I was being mean. I think I was being honest and factually accurate," she says of her family, relationships with black and white friends and colleagues, plus *The Post* experience. The book weaves Ms. Nelson's personal struggle with class, race and relationship issues into a sometimes painful, often very funny chronicle of an African-American professional's failure to succeed in a white-owned corporation. A few chapters into the memoir, it is apparent that her encounters are emblematic of those faced by blacks who work across America's corporate landscape, inside such venerable institutions as law firms, banks and manufacturing companies.

The American Bar Association Journal, for example, in an article this year, reported that more than one-third of minority law partners have departed major Chicago firms since 1991. The ABA used the Chicago study to take a broader look at what is happening to blacks in law firms nationally.

A local example of the frustrations Ms. Nelson says she experienced is Dallas lawyer Aaron Wiley, 28, an assistant prosecutor with the Dallas County district attorney's office. Mr. Wiley says he quit a blue-chip law firm when it became apparent that he would not receive the grooming or the opportunities to pursue his goal of trying cases.

Of his experience, he says: "It was like a maze with three rats. There was a little black rat, a little white rat and a big white rat. The black rat keeps running into closed doors, and the big white rat whispers to the little white rat: 'Turn left, turn right.'

"At the end of the day, the white rat is said to be intelligent, smart and filled with initiative, and the black rat lacks initiative, is not goal-oriented and is unintelligent."

Craig K. Polite, a New York clinical psychologist who has treated dozens of black professionals in his booming Manhattan practice, says many blacks, especially middle-class blacks, are unprepared for

> 'It was like a maze with three rats... The black rat keeps running into closed doors, and the big white rat whispers to the little white rat, "Turn left, turn right."'

the realities of corporate life.

Dr. Polite, who has studied black success in corporate life, says some blacks refuse to accept the true nature of corporate culture, a refusal that can lead to depression, anger and self-destructive behavior.

"Many of my clients really expected that just because their degree said Harvard, they could somehow transcend the B.S.," Dr. Polite says. "They didn't understand that corporations are often as vicious and idiosyncratic as knife fights."

Ms. Nelson says she, too, was wounded on the corporate battlefield.

"It was my trial by fire, my defining moment. You have to have an enormous amount of strength to survive the corporate culture." Still, she says, her account is "not a victim book. It's about a contemporary African-American woman who made choices, some that worked out, some that didn't."

That many didn't work out during her tumultuous tenure doesn't bother Ms. Nelson now.

'A lot of things happened to Jill that a lot of people in the newsroom can identify with.'

■ ■ ■ ■ ■ ■ ■ ■ ■ ■

"I learned a lot," she says. "And I got a great book out of it." *Volunteer Slavery* is an incisive, often damning account of the cost of assimilation.

Milton Coleman, assistant managing editor of *The Post*, says "*Volunteer Slavery* is first and foremost Jill's story of what she brought to *The Post* and what she got out of it."

Mr. Coleman, one of Ms. Nelson's former supervisors, adds: "I do not feel as though she stretched the truth to fit her story. I think she did a responsible journalist's job. A lot of things happened to Jill that a lot of people in the newsroom can identify with. Other things were truly Jill's take on them."

When Ms. Nelson asserted herself at work, she writes, she was "treated like a great, big, intimidating Negress, so I spend half my time trying to make myself nonthreatening, even though I'm not really threatening, so the Caucasians can deal with me even though it's not really me they feel threatened by, it's their image of me ..."

When she writes of the dual responsibilities of African-American journalists, she strikes a chord for most black professionals. African Americans are, "like their Caucasian colleagues, dedicated, hard-working professionals trying to play by the rules and move up in the system. The difference is that where white reporters have one job, black reporters have several.

"Not only must we function as reporters, but we are also ambassadors from that colored catch-all, Black America, explaining and justifying not only ourselves but also the mythical, monolithic 'black community.'"

The outspoken Ms. Nelson has few regrets about leaving a $60,000-a-year job. And she's not worried about whether her memoir will burn bridges.

"My career is better than ever," she says triumphantly. "You wouldn't believe the people calling up asking me to write for them."

Personally, Ms. Nelson says, she is exactly where she wants to be.

"Here I am back living a charmed life again. I am a free person. I've gotten to be No. 1 to myself. I am doing the work that I love, being around the people that I love. Life is not about cash, bylines, prestige, access or any of the things a job may or may not offer," she says. "I know it sounds corny and New Age-y, but that's the way I feel."

As it turned out, *The Washington Post* wasn't the end of Ms. Nelson's uncomfortable contact with America's corporate powers. *Volunteer Slavery* was rejected by 32 mainstream publishers before Noble Press, a tiny, progressive Chicago publisher known for socially and environmentally conscious books, accepted it. "The more mainstream publishers were not used to that voice, especially coming from a black person, especially an African-American woman," Ms. Nelson says.

Released last month, *Volunteer Slavery* is already in its third printing, which proves that her message is universal, that her book isn't just for blacks, Ms. Nelson says.

"A few white men over 50 who run institutions of all kinds have declared themselves the masters of the universe and told the rest of us that we're crazy, incompetent or demanding because we're black, we're Latino, we're women," Ms. Nelson says.

"We are the mainstream, and I'm not going anywhere. This book touches a lot of people," she says. "A 45-year-old white man called me up and said: 'I'm a volunteer slave, too.'"

July 21, 1993

A Professor's Passion

■ ■ ■ ■ ■ ■ ■ ■ ■ ■

Cornel West looks like everybody's image of an academic or a hip preacher, circa 1970. He favors out-of-style, slightly large three-piece suits, oversized glasses and a fluffy 'Fro, passe in this era of fades, dreadlocks and custom-cut designer suits. While he looks as though he is oblivious to fashion, friends say Dr. West's is a carefully cultivated image. People who might bristle at the radical elements of this Princeton University professor's message are disarmed by a man who resembles a benign soul saver, who spouts pointed political, economic and social messages with the whispered and rumbled oratory of a black Protestant cleric.

"West claims he's never been called to preaching, but he's been preaching all along," says Dr. Derek Harkins, pastor of New Hope Baptist Church in South Dallas.

During an eight-hour Dallas visit recently, Dr. West, 40, makes a morning appointment, eats lunch, promotes his best-selling new book on a radio talk show, hurries to a book signing through rush-hour traffic, then dashes to the airport, barely catching his flight back to Detroit. The philosopher's high-octane life (he gives more than 75 off-campus lectures each semester) has become a series of one-day engagements since the April 29 publication of *Race Matters*, his eighth and most popularly embraced book.

"I've been on the move, no doubt about it," he says. "It's put me behind on so many other projects."

Most of the essays in *Race Matters* (Beacon Press) appeared first in anthologies, general interest publications and academic journals as diverse as *The New York Times Magazine, Dissent, Tikkun, Emerge* and *Z Magazine*.

The wide spectrum of publications reflects Dr. West's obsession with provoking dialogue across class, color and religious lines.

"I'm trying to deal with misunderstandings and miscommunications by focusing on fundamental social change," he says earnestly. "My friends say, 'Corn, you have too much hope.' I tell them, 'I'm not an optimist, you know. I'm full of hope, but I'm not an optimist.'"

The 105-page book, through its eight essays, offers analysis of black nihilism, black-Jewish relations, Malcolm X and his appeal to angry black youth, black conservatives and black leadership. For example, in the chapter "Demystifying the New Black Conservatism," Dr. West discusses black conservatives and affirmative action:

"Mobility by means of affirmative action breeds tenuous self-respect and questionable peer acceptance for middle-class blacks. The new black conservatives voiced these feelings in the form of attacks on affirmative action programs (despite the fact that they had achieved their positions by means of such programs).

'My friends say, "Corn, you have too much hope.' I tell them... 'I'm full of hope, but I'm not an optimist."'

"... But the black conservatives overlook the fact that affirmative action policies were political responses to the pervasive refusal of most white Americans to judge black Americans on that basis. The new black conservatives assume that without affirmative action programs, white Americans will make choices on merit rather than on race. Yet they have adduced no evidence for this ..."

His publishers released *Race Matters* on the first anniversary of the Los Angeles riots and sent Dr. West to the city, where he was a sought-after analyst for the local and national media. The timely book has catapulted the Harvard-educated Dr. West, the grandson of a Baptist minister, into immense popularity.

Beacon Press quickly sold out of its 45,000 first printing, and the book is already in its sixth run. It has remained on *The New York Times* best-seller list for five consecutive weeks, and its paperback rights were sold to Vintage for $175,000, one of the largest rights sales in Beacon's history. Customers at Black Images Book Bazaar in Dallas are responding in similar fashion, says Emma Rodgers, co-owner of the store.

Dr. Harkins of the New Hope Baptist Church in South Dallas, who studied under Dr. West at Union Theological Seminary during the early 1980s, says he is thrilled to see his former professor spreading the gospel outside academia.

"It's fabulous that he is exposing a broader group of people to piercing thought about race, culture society and class," Dr. Harkins says.

Long an in-demand college speaker, Dr. West also finds his sudden celebrity unexpected. So many speaking requests pour in, he has hired a booking agent to schedule engagements. Asked why he thinks the book is so popular, Dr. West shrugs.

"A lot of folks, black folk and white folk, genuinely are interested in reconciliation," Dr. West says. "There are people, all kinds of people, who realize that all forms of oppression are a plague on this society."

Dr. West is fascinating to watch. Autograph seekers at Black Images speed through the line. Rather than pausing to chat with him individually, they grab chairs, create an impromptu congregation and wait for a sermon. When Dr. West sheepishly announces that he can speak for maybe 10 minutes, no one grumbles.

He smiles, then launches into an extemporaneous talk about morality and its role in everyday life. The group stares at him, nodding in agreement.

Dr. West is characteristically humble about people's response to him.

"I'm just my mama's child," he says. "I just want people to understand that the situation of black people is integral to the situation of America, that issues of race and class are not marginal or ghettoize-able."

Best-selling biographer Arnold Rampersad, one of Dr. West's Princeton colleagues, says he didn't expect *Race Matters* to draw so many readers.

"It's not the easiest book in the world to read," Dr. Rampersad says. "It must be what Cornel says all the time — that there is a reservoir of good will in this country that remains unexhausted, that many people are interested in solving the problems of race and economic injustice."

Dr. Rampersad attributes the West phenomenon to his colleague's brilliance, charisma and unwavering dedication to building interracial coalitions.

"He's committed to genuine intellectual exchange," Dr. Rampersad says. "You cannot say that about a lot of cultural critics or contemporary theorists. Many are fueled simply by an ideologically arrogant dedication to their own point of view.

"When people hear and meet Cornel, they realize they're being schooled," Dr. Rampersad continues. "It is an exhilarating experience.

"If you have lunch with Cornel, you'd better pick a spot outside of the county because he will stop to talk with 15 or 16 people along the way," Dr. Rampersad adds. "He goes out of his way not to avoid contact with people."

July 13, 1993

SECTION II

.

HISTORY
LESSONS

....

Freedman's Memories

■ ■ ■ ■ ■ ■ ■ ■ ■ ■

The earth-movers digging at the corner of Lemmon Avenue and Central Expressway in Dallas lay bare the rotting wood that conceals the dry bones — and so much more.

As the machines scrape away, inch by inch, the dust that has hidden the bodies of former slaves, their children and their children's children, the memories are surfacing, too — sparse, fragmented but charged with longing.

All over Dallas, African Americans are whispering in wistful voices and searching for old scrapbooks and photo albums, tenuous links to a life almost, but not quite, forgotten. The photographs, some as old as the century itself, show a world self-contained and self-sufficient, cut off from the opportunities but also from the enmity of white Dallas.

African Americans shop in dry-goods stores owned and run by other African Americans. Men strut down the streets, their Thom McAn shoes shining in the afternoon sun. Families sit for formal portraits in front of fireplaces, and business-suited leaders pose proudly at civic and social club functions.

"North Dallas was one of the largest black settlements in the South," says Dr. Mamie McKnight, president and founder of Black Dallas Remembered, a historical preservation group. "It was a self-contained community of black-owned businesses and institutions — some say more than we have now."

Freedman's Town, or Old North Dallas as it's sometimes called, was bounded by Leonard Street and McKinney, Washington and Ross avenues. Freedman's Cemetery, then the Colored Cemetery, sat at Lemmon Avenue and Campbell Street, forming a grassy barrier between black and white Dallas.

Robert Prince, 60, a physician and lay historian descended from one of Dallas' oldest black families, says about 300 former slaves settled around the cemetery, which appears to have existed before the Civil War. Looking for opportunity, they came to Dallas from the Galveston area and points in the Deep South. Sales records indicate that the burial ground and land near it were unsuitable for farming and, therefore, might have been undesirable to white residents. Jobs were scarce for the former slaves. But in the 1870s, construction of the Houston and Texas Central Railroad brought the first wave of economic progress to their community, according to Dr. Prince.

'People aren't told that black Americans laid the railroad tracks that made this town prosper.'

▪ ▪ ▪ ▪ ▪ ▪ ▪ ▪ ▪ ▪

"People aren't told that black Americans laid the railroad track that made this town prosper," he says. "Dallas would have been like Waxahachie if it hadn't been for us."

During the first decades of the 20th century, the trains that traveled those tracks were tended by African-American porters. Income from the coveted porter positions elevated the men's families to the city's early black middle class, says Emerson Emory, a psychiatrist whose father ran numbers for local mobsters.

But affluent or impoverished, all blacks lived side by side within the confines of Freedman's Town. Dr. Emory says his family, always in search of cheap rent, lived in a succession of flats around Freedman's Cemetery. One of Dr. Emory's friends, Dallas lawyer Louis Bedford, lived in a two-story house paid for, in part, by his father's earnings as a cook.

"People who did have a little something, there was no place else for them to live," Dr. Emory says. "We all sort of associated with each other."

Those who had the money watched motion pictures at their own movie house, the Harlem Theater on Elm Street near the railroad tracks. A few years later, they would go to the State Theater, at the intersection of Thomas Avenue and Hall Street. Even after blacks began settling in Oak Cliff, South Dallas and other areas of the city, activities and institutions rooted in North Dallas continued to attract African Americans from other areas. Until the late 1940s, the community offered the only public library open to blacks.

Residents ordered hats from black haberdashers, had their hair cut by black barbers, attended neighborhood schools and buried their dead in Freedman's Cemetery, which operated from 1861 through 1925. The sick sought care at Bluitt Sanitarium, a small hospital owned by an African-American doctor.

Segregation was so completely entrenched that survivors from the era can't remember seeing many white people.

"Italians owned some grocery stores," says Dr. Emory. "We played with their children. Otherwise we didn't mix. We didn't ask why. That's just the way things were."

Within the black community, the bonds were strong — and so was the discipline. Children were fed by their families and nurtured by all adults. Any child who misbehaved could count on adult witnesses to report the indiscretion to his or her parents, often before he or she could get home.

"If you were unruly, almost any adult in the neighborhood would whup you," Mr. Bedford says. "If you were out late, you were working — or running an errand on a bicycle."

Back then, an urban childhood retained its innocence, Mr. Bedford says. Neighborhood boys played in the cemetery. They chose the graveyard he says, because bullies often picked fights in nearby Griggs Park, the one public play area open to black children. The lawyer, now 64, passed many a day in the cemetery playing hide-and-seek and rubber gun, a fast-paced form of tag that involved shooting opponents with pieces of bicycle inner tube.

Frances Burns, a retired social worker, grew up in the 1930s on Cochran Street, a few blocks from the graveyard. Her most vivid memory of it comes from an encounter with a childhood foe, a neighborhood girl who would bury slips of paper containing the names of playmates she was mad at. News of a "burial" spread quickly.

"One night, somebody stopped by to tell us she'd buried my

name," says Mrs. Burns, chuckling at the incident that angered and frightened her 50 years ago.

At the turn of the century, some affluent black families educated their children in Corsicana, a town south of Dallas that was said to have better schools, Dr. McKnight says.

Of those who were educated in Dallas, the most fortunate lived close to the Dallas Colored High School, says Alvernon Tripp, a 1915 graduate. On Cochran, across from the cemetery, the school employed graduates of black colleges to teach students in first through 12th grades.

Teen-agers who lived in settlements on the outskirts of town took whatever transportation was available to the high school in Old North Dallas. Others walked the dirt roads from what were then rural areas and are now part of West Dallas and South Dallas. Children whose families couldn't afford transportation — and there were many — just didn't go to school.

Educated or not, residents of Old North Dallas knew the latest about employment opportunities in the North, lynchings across the South and the doings of personalities such as W.E.B. Du Bois and the poet Paul Laurence Dunbar.

They got their news from African-American-owned tabloids such as the *Brotherhood Eyes* and more staid black-owned publications such as *The Dallas Express, The Houston Informer* and even *The Pittsburgh Courier, The Chicago Defender* and New York City's *Amsterdam News*. Because Dallas' white-owned dailies rarely chronicled events in the city's minority communities, enterprising African-American boys walked door to door, peddling the papers that published the information blacks craved.

One day, the news was about the Freedman's Cemetery. Louise Cowens, 78, a retired singer, still can picture the public notice, printed in the 1930s, that offered $10 to residents who claimed bodies buried in the Colored Cemetery. The advertisement marked the first of several major road projects that eventually would all but obliterate the cemetery and the surrounding community.

Ms. Cowens, her mother and her five siblings had often visited the graveyard to pay homage to her maternal grandfather, Mack

McCoy. Her grandfather had supported his family by cutting hair in a barbershop on Akard Street between Elm and San Jacinto streets. Although he died before Ms. Cowens was born, she proudly displays his portrait in her Oak Cliff living room.

"Mama would take us up there, but she didn't exactly know where he was," Ms. Cowens says. "When I went by there (after the disinterment started) and saw them digging those people up, it hurt my heart. They had those boxes stacked up yay-high, five or six high. There were oodles of 'em. I knew Grandfather was one they were digging up."

By the 1940s, few members of the next generation of African Americans would even know that slaves and former slaves were buried beneath the wild irises and overgrown weeds.

By the 1940s, few members of the next generation would even know slaves and former slaves were buried here.

"There were no markers," Mrs. Burns says. "I never remember there being any tombstones."

Although Old North Dallas remained the heart of the black community, former residents had begun to find jobs and establish neighborhoods in other parts of the city, and to use businesses and cemeteries closer to their new homes. African Americans who migrated to California and Northern cities took their memories with them. Eventually, only a few dozen people paid much attention to the old cemetery.

In 1965, a committee of African Americans descended from people buried in the cemetery petitioned the city, successfully, to designate it Freedman's Park.

Those committee members, all dead, might well be pleased to know that the graveyard's fate is now a matter of interest to publications as far-flung as *The New York Times* and *The Economist* of London. State law prohibits the highway department from continuing the widening of Central Expressway until all the bodies in the path of the expansion have been removed. Officials initially expected to reinter about 150 caskets from a strip of land that runs along the west frontage road. But recent archaeological work has discovered an estimated 600 bodies beneath Lemmon Avenue, Calvary Drive and the planned right-of-way.

More than 150 Dallas residents — old and young, black and white — gathered recently at City Hall to discuss the cemetery's future and remember its past. About 20 people have volunteered to research death certificates for Black Dallas Remembered.

"For 10 years, I've tried to get the name changed," to reflect the park's history as a cemetery, says Dr. Prince. "I tried to get money raised for a monument. Finally, I feel gratified that in the 50 years since the land was taken for Central Expressway, the sensitivity of the community has evolved to a much higher level."

But he's not about to relax his vigilance.

"I think it's sacrilegious to disturb the final resting place of my ancestors. My grandfather borrowed $300 to keep that cemetery up, and it's my duty to keep watch," he says.

"I feel very strongly that I could be one of those individuals reincarnated."

October 21, 1990

Experiment
in Pain
■ ■ ■ ■ ■ ■ ■ ■ ■ ■

L eroy McDonald was just beginning his film career when he took a 10-minute break that would influence his work for the next 19 years.

The date was July 26, 1972. Mr. McDonald was a film student, working as an intern on a movie and wondering what to choose as the topic for his thesis film, when a crew member handed him that day's *New York Times*. At the bottom of page one, beneath the story of Democratic vice-presidential nominee Thomas Eagleton's admission that he had undergone electric shock therapy for depression, was an Associated Press story about a U.S. government experiment called the Tuskegee Study of Untreated Syphilis in the Negro Male.

The article described how, over a period of 40 years, the U.S. Public Health Service had documented the suffering of nearly 400 poor, black syphilis patients while not giving them drugs to combat the disease.

"The story was on the front page, in the bottom left-hand corner," says Mr. McDonald, who grew up in Texarkana, Texas. "It was small, very small. The study didn't get much attention."

The experiment clung to Mr. McDonald's memory, though. It became the subject of his thesis film and provided him with a lifetime cause. Today, he is trying to raise $5 million for a feature film about the project.

The study began in 1932. Public Health Service doctors from Washington and Atlanta used promises of hot meals, $50 burial stipends and free treatment to induce the black men of Tuskegee, Ala., to submit to blood tests, according to *Bad Blood*, a book that chronicles the experiment.

Men who tested positive for syphilis were invited to join a special health care program that offered free annual physicals and a cure for "bad blood." The subjects, mostly sharecroppers, were not told that they were part of a study or that they had a deadly disease that could infect their wives and unborn children, says Fred Gray of Tuskegee, a civil rights lawyer who in 1974 won a $10 million settlement for the subjects and their heirs. Untreated, syphilis leads to blindness, heart disease and severe neurological damage.

The subjects were not told that they .... had a deadly disease that could infect their wives and unborn children.

▪ ▪ ▪ ▪ ▪ ▪ ▪ ▪ ▪ ▪

Public Health Service researchers conducted annual "roundups" of the syphilitic men and, from the outset, asked local doctors not to test or treat the subjects, says James Jones, the University of Houston history professor who wrote *Bad Blood*. Local physicians, not wishing to interfere with the agency's research, gave no care to the infected men. During the roundups, federal doctors "treated" the men with aspirin if they complained of aches and pains, according to congressional testimony.

Although treatment was available for syphilis when the experiment began, Public Health Service researchers claimed that the risks outweighed the benefits, says Dr. Vernal G. Cave, a venereal disease expert. Penicillin came into use as a cure for syphilis in the 1940s — roughly a decade after the experiment began — but none was administered to the test subjects, and many of them died of the disease.

Dr. Cave, now in private practice in New York City, served on the government committee that recommended stopping the experiment after the AP story broke in 1972. He says the panel voted unanimously to destroy the records of its findings, including taped interviews with principals.

In 1958, the Public Health Service awarded the survivors certificates "in grateful recognition of 25 years of active participation in the Tuskegee medical research study" plus $1 for every year of service.

Between 1936 and 1973, 13 accounts of the study were published in medical journals. The articles, with titles such as "Untreated Syphilis in the Male Negro: Observation of Abnormalities Over Sixteen Years" and "The Tuskegee Study of Untreated Syphilis: The 30th Year of Observation," revealed that no new information was being generated by the study.

"Researchers simply decided to withhold treatment to see what the germ would do to the human body," says the federal review panel's Dr. Cave. "They didn't discover anything new. Examining the records, we realized how careless the government was in all of this. It was unscientific. Autopsies were conducted under poor conditions. No one even asked, "Hey, why are we doing this?'" Says Dr. Jones, the author: "The study took on a life of its own."

How could such a thing have happened?

"You have to take in the context of time," says Mr. Gray, the lawyer. "It was rural Alabama, 1932."

In a community where residents were extremely poor, undernourished and often chronically ill, the death rate of the experiment subjects may not have appeared unusual, says Mr. Gray, who gained fame defending Rosa Parks and the Rev. Martin Luther King Jr.

"These were black men with no formal education," Mr. Gray says. "Many had never seen a doctor, much less been treated by one. Anything white people asked them to do, they did."

Today, even well-informed, well-educated people seem to have trouble comprehending the experiment, says Dr. Jones, who spent seven years researching *Bad Blood*, published by a division of Macmillan in 1981.

Mention of the study frequently elicits protests of disbelief, stony silence, plain shock or diatribes of misinformation, the historian says. "One misconception is that government doctors gave syphilis to the subjects,' he says. "Another misconception is that the experiment was a secret."

The Tuskegee study has become a rallying point among African Americans who have long believed in the existence of a conspiracy to exterminate black people, says Frances Cress-Welsing, a Washington psychiatrist, prolific writer on issues of race and frequent *Nightline* guest.

She says the study was a form of racial genocide and compares it to experiments used on Jews in Nazi Germany.

"That might play into why there were 400 black men," Dr. Welsing says. "Men generally are the people who initiate sexual intercourse. By using men, the perpetrators ensured that the disease would spread."

Tuskegee Subject No. 626, Leroy McDonald's 52-minute film about the experiment, is a fictionalized account of how the untreated disease affects one couple's marriage and causes their infant to be stillborn.

Mr. McDonald says he used composite characters and changed some details because the class-action suit against the government was being litigated when he shot his movie.

Now, nearly 20 years after producing and editing *Tuskegee Subject No. 626*, the 49-year-old film maker is determined to raise funds to make a full-length feature about the syphilis study.

But Hollywood already has displayed a skittishness about the subject, according to Dr. Jones, who was approached about a film after the publication of *Bad Blood*.

"The book has been optioned by big-name producers several times," Mr. Jones says. "It's a very hard film to get through the Hollywood and television hierarchies. Projects always have died at the vice-presidential level. Each time a turndown came, the explanation was always that the story is so unrelentingly grim. Who's going to argue with that?"

Those rejections are fine with Mr. McDonald, who reasons that the longer the studios put off making a film, the better his opportunities for making one. Besides, he believes Hollywood will ruin the story by downplaying the role of racism.

"A studio will tell me to take the guts out," Mr. McDonald says. "They will have me make it palatable to whites."

Determined to tell the story from the black perspective, Mr. McDonald has spent the last 18 months criss-crossing the country, drumming up support among affluent and politically active blacks. Screenings of *Tuskegee Subject No. 626* in Oakland, Calif., and Atlanta have attracted investors. He hopes the movie will stimulate a similar response among potential investors in the Dallas area.

To "comfortably" make the movie, he estimates, will cost a minimum of $5 million. He says he has promises of in-kind services and cash commitments equal to about 5 percent of that sum.

After seeing *Miss Evers' Boys*, a 1989 play loosely based on the facts of the experiment, Mr. McDonald says he is more determined than ever to tell the story.

The stage drama focuses on a black nurse at Tuskegee who acted as liaison between the subjects and the government. The character resembles Eunice Rivers Laurie, a black nurse employed to oversee the study from 1932 until her 1965 retirement.

The playwright "made the black nurse the culprit," Mr. McDonald says. "Again, the government got off the hook."

Dr. Daniel Feldshuh, a Cornell University theater professor and an emergency room physician, objects to Mr. McDonald's characterization of his drama, winner of the 1989 New American Play Award.

"Actually, I see the nurse as a victim, not a culprit," Dr. Feldshuh says. "The play attempts to show how she was a woman caught in the middle of a man's world, a nurse trapped in a doctor's world and a black in a white world.

"With all due respect to Mr. McDonald, to suggest that I suggested she was culpable would be to ignore the overwhelming role of institutional and scientific racism," says Dr. Feldshuh, who is white. "I was trying to understand her, not blame her. If you just read the facts, certainly she is less sympathetic than she is in the play."

> '... She was a woman caught in the middle of a man's world, a nurse trapped in a doctor's world and a black in a white world.'
>
> ■ ■ ■ ■ ■ ■ ■ ■ ■ ■ ■

According to Mr. Jones' book, Ms. Laurie and other Tuskegee-area health-care professionals cooperated with the government by agreeing not to treat the subjects. But Mr. Gray, who represented the men and their families, says Tuskegee's black medical professionals were themselves misled, possibly believing that the federal doctors were treating the men's syphilis during their yearly visits. Medical records and other information about the study were kept in Atlanta.

Says Mr. Gray: "I'm not sure any of them knew in any detail what was going on."

April 2, 1991

Radical Changes

■ ■ ■ ■ ■ ■ ■ ■ ■ ■

B lack Power. All Power to the People. Death to the Pigs. A quarter of a century has passed since those words, shouted by members of the Black Panther Party, often marching military-style down the streets, frightened white America.

In Dallas, as in Los Angeles, where there was a December 1969 shootout with police, the Panthers' combativeness and open contempt for law enforcement officials made them synonymous in the minds of many with violence and racial hatred. Many national Panther leaders, 28 in all, died during police raids in Chicago and other cities. Others, such as Bobby Seale, Bobby Rush and the late Huey Newton, were imprisoned. Eventually, FBI infiltrators destroyed the party and turned many of its surviving members against one another.

Lost in the reverberations of the gun battles was the Panthers' basic message.

■ ■ ■ ■ ■ ■ ■ ■ ■ ■

Lost in the reverberations of the gun battles was the Panthers' basic message, a message of economic self-determination, community involvement and citizen control of local institutions, including police.

But as former Panthers across the nation commemorate the 25th anniversary of the party's birth, several former Panthers are still here in Dallas, quietly working, each in his own way, for those very goals. The onetime Panther weapons expert is a member of the city's crime prevention unit. The organizer of a Panther campaign against sickle cell anemia promotes AIDS education for the county. The founder of a Panther "liberation school" pastors a Fort Worth church. The firebrand who railed against police brutality spearheads grass-roots anti-drug efforts in South Dallas.

They and others gathered in October 1991, for a 25th-anniversary program. The event — complete with a video presentation, short speeches and a display of photos and newspaper clippings from the party's short-lived heyday in Dallas — seemed more like a reunion of Boy Scouts than Black Panthers. But one member, Fahim Minkah, leader of the Dallas Black Panther Party from 1973 to 1977, disputes the history of the local group and questions whether some reunion participants were actually party members.

Nevertheless, each man said that his years as a Panther had left profound marks on his life.

"Ours is an important story that needs to be corrected," says the Rev. LeRoy Haynes, a charter member of the first Dallas group, the National Committee to Combat Fascism. "The Panther name sometimes frightens people. It shouldn't."

■ Preaching empowerment

Khaleef Rasul Hasan grew up an Army brat, and in those days he was known as Charles Paul Henderson. The only thing worse than being a military brat, he says, was being a black military brat in segregated military towns.

"On military bases, the black kids always banded together," says Mr. Hasan, 48. "We'd fight all the time. Whenever there was trouble, the police would always come to the black kids. That's where I developed a sense of injustice."

When he wasn't fighting or playing with friends, he was firing or tearing apart and reassembling all kinds of weapons.

He returned to Dallas after getting expelled from the University of Kansas for fighting with a security guard. At Kansas, he had studied political science and military science. When the Dallas affiliate of the Black Panther Party formed during the summer of 1970, he served as defense captain. "I knew about guns and things. I knew about military tactics. I knew how to shoot and I could teach the others the whole works."

Central headquarters purged the Dallas affiliate shortly after it was sanctioned in 1971, because the group had been infiltrated by an FBI informant, according to news reports from the era. Mr. Hasan moved to California, where he ran the East Oakland chapter and became security adviser at central headquarters in Oakland.

It was a course some of his friends back home just couldn't fathom. "We're way apart on ideology," says Walter Travis, executive director of the Washington Street Presbyterian Mission in Dallas. "But Charles made me look at the Panthers differently.

"A lot of black leadership, they go back and forth on the issues. He (Mr. Hasan) is very loyal to his beliefs. Then and now, he made rounds to a lot of the community centers. He has a lot of respect for people whether they are moderate, conservative or liberal. Very few people I know respect others the way he does."

Mr. Hasan, a crime-prevention representative for Dallas, still preaches black empowerment. He continues to draw his inspiration from Malcolm X, who, like him, derived much of his philosophy from the teachings of Islam.

And he remains proud of the Panthers' accomplishments. "We helped get (California congressman) Ron Dellums elected," he says. "We got the hooks (hoodlums) off the streets. If the Panthers were still around, we wouldn't have the drug problems we have today."

Seven years as a Black Panther taught him, he says, "that issues are not just black and white. I learned that they are right or wrong."

■ A 'thinker'

Sickle cell anemia kept James "Skip" Shockley out of the military at a time when few civilian jobs were offered to young, unskilled black men. So, as the Black Power movement began creeping into Dallas during the late '60s, Mr. Shockley found himself doing the same things he sees a lot of young black men doing today.

"I was hanging around the streets," he says. "I was unemployed."

He met LeRoy Haynes, then a student leader enrolled at El Centro Community College. Mr. Haynes asked him to join a fledgling affiliate chapter of the Black Panther Party. He agreed.

"He's a thinker," says Charles Wyatt of San Diego, Mr. Shockley's older brother. "The Panthers gave him goals to achieve as a black person who wants to better his community."

Because much of the activism was centered on campus, Mr. Shockley says he enrolled at El Centro Community College "but didn't go to class." Instead, he helped set up a free clothing distribution program and developed a neighborhood program for sickle cell testing.

'The party gave me a sense of family, I learned to live with others and to be responsible — not just for me, but for everyone.'

■ ■ ■ ■ ■ ■ ■ ■ ■ ■

After the Dallas chapter was purged, he moved to Denton, Texas, and then to Houston, where he recruited medical students to donate time to the Panthers' free medical clinics. With the national leadership decimated by death and imprisonment, Mr. Shockley and other Houston members were called to Oakland headquarters in 1973 to assume leadership positions.

In California, he helped direct a day-care center and run medical programs. "I taught, baby-sat, developed curriculum and drove buses," Mr. Shockley says.

He put that experience to work when he returned home in 1975. "When I came back (to Dallas), I got a job in day care," Mr. Shockley says. "It was time to start a new life."

He built much of that new life around a commitment to public health. A registered nurse, he counsels clients in the Dallas County Health Department AIDS education program and is working toward a degree in community health at Texas Woman's University. He is married to a pharmacist.

A small, soft-spoken man, Mr. Shockley, 44, says his participation in the Black Panther Party had a profound effect on the choices he's made since.

"The party gave me a sense of family," he says. "I learned to live with others and to be responsible — not just for me, but for everyone."

■ Journey to a pulpit

Betty Johnson knows that college has a way of changing people. But that knowledge in no way prepared her for the man her younger brother became after he left Beaumont, Texas, in 1967 to enroll in a joint University of Texas at Austin/Houston-Tillotson College program.

The man who is now the Rev. LeRoy Haynes started spouting the philosophies of Chairman Mao and other radical leaders whose theories he first encountered in his textbooks.

"I was praying for him to get out of that," says Ms. Johnson, a Pentecostal evangelist. "It was changing him."

Activism was familiar to the Haynes children: They had participated in sit-ins during the early years of the Civil Rights Movement. What startled Mr. Haynes' family was his leadership in the National Committee to Combat Fascism, the Dallas affiliate of the Black Panther Party.

When the party expelled the Dallas group, Mr. Haynes took a group to Denton, where he enrolled as a political science student at North Texas State University (now the University of North Texas). He continued his community organizing with another Panther affiliate, the Black Intercommunal Party.

The group established "survival programs" for black Denton residents, including a free breakfast program, a voter registration drive and a "liberation school" for 70 black children. The organizers financed the programs with their scholarship money, contributions from white donors, fund-raising dances, newspaper sales and stipends sent by unsuspecting parents.

"Denton was an example of how you could go into a community and organize it from the bottom up," Mr. Haynes says.

Few people who know Mr. Haynes now would recognize him in the 1972 newspaper photo that shows him, in striped bell-bottoms, a wide-lapeled shirt and a thick Afro, selling Black Panther Party newspapers outside the student union.

The Black Panther Party, says Mr. Haynes, propelled him in many unexpected ways. He ran for the Denton City Council in 1973. He earned honors as a student at North Texas and later at Southern Methodist University's Perkins School of Theology.

Mr. Haynes, 42, is married to psychologist and radio talk-show host Brenda Wall. He commits his free time to progressive community organizations such as the Common Ground Community Economic Development Corp.

But he has transferred his preaching from the streets to the pulpit of Carter Metropolitan Christian Methodist Episcopal Church in southeast Fort Worth. It was, he says, a radical move in a lifetime of radical moves. Everyone expected him to go to law school. "They were shocked when I told them I was going to go to seminary."

▪ Few regrets

Fahim Minkah was like lava that flowed unabated. Nearly every time the members of the Dallas City Council looked up, he stood at the microphone, lambasting them about injustice to black people, poor people and anyone else he felt was oppressed.

In April 1974, six months after Mr. Minkah re-established the Dallas chapter of the Black Panther Party, a lead story in *The Black Panther* — the national party's newspaper — told readers how vengeful officials with a legal services organization were trying to squeeze Mr. Minkah out of his paralegal job.

"Life was miserable then," Mr. Minkah says. "If I dwelled on what I went through personally, I'd be a very bitter man."

A year later, fist thrust into the air, Mr. Minkah, then Fred Bell, made the cover again, this time for leading a group of 1,000 demonstrators through the streets of downtown Dallas. He says his unflinching stands were met with police surveillance, several arrests and mounting legal entanglements, many relating to a 1968 conviction for aiding and abetting the robbery of a Ladonia, Texas, bank. Mr. Minkah served a four-year sentence in the federal penitentiary at Leavenworth, Kan., in connection with the robbery.

"I had to carry a pistol all the time," Mr. Minkah remembers. "We had to put our mattresses on the floor because the floor was where we felt most protected."

Undeterred, Mr. Minkah, now 52, continued to storm into city council meetings to deliver impromptu speeches and lists of demands throughout the mid-'70s. Under his leadership, the Dallas chapter initiated boycotts of merchants, pest control services, tenant organizations, free legal clinics and a host of other programs. One issue, lobbying for the establishment of a citizen-run police review board, kept activists occupied long after the chapter disbanded in 1977.

To this day, Mr. Minkah insists that he organized the first and only chapter of the Black Panther Party in Dallas. But in late 1970, police reports identified Mr. Hasan, the late Curtis Gaines and others as Black Panther Party leaders. Also, Stuart Hanlon, a San Francisco lawyer for Elmer "Geronimo" Pratt, a Panther leader still imprisoned on a murder charge, says his client came to Texas in 1970 to help organize and supervise the Dallas Panthers.

The National Committee to Combat Fascism never was a chapter, Mr. Minkah says. "The leadership was party members. It never was a branch. I never said it wasn't associated with the party. It was.

"Before I knew anything, Khaleef and them were calling this reunion," Mr. Minkah explains. "When he told me who was doing it, I said, 'Well, they weren't Panthers.'"

For Mr. Minkah, the toll was economic. Old newspaper articles show that he regularly fought to be rehired to jobs he was fired from, mostly in city-run or non-profit social service agencies. A single father of four, he is now program director for the Dallas chapter of the Black United Front, a community services group. He is a founder of African-American Men Against Narcotics, which organizes marches and other activities designed to force drug dealers out of black neighborhoods.

He says he has few regrets.

"The party showed me that you can't uplift the community with rhetoric alone," Mr. Minkah says. "It allowed me to test (political) theories. It helped me learn about the rights of the people. It helped me develop a method to share that information. It showed me that useful programs, programs that meet people's needs, get the people organized."

October 30, 1991

Cultivating
a Dream

■■■■■■■■■■

ROCKETT, Texas — Red Kitchen poses with his Simmental bull on a poster printed by the state Agriculture Department. The look on Mr. Kitchen's face is confident, as befits his success. But one element of that success makes the black rancher uncomfortable: He's snapped up cattle and land lost by other African Americans.

Across the nation, thousands of black farmers can barely come up with the cash to plant seed. But through meticulous planning and conservative spending, Mr. Kitchen, 62, has amassed thousands of acres in this community 80 miles northeast of Houston.

The rancher's ability to buy land makes him an anomaly among black farmers. "I went to the Army a couple of years, got back and decided I wanted me some land," Mr. Kitchen says. "I'd hate to see us all end up on concrete someday."

'I wanted me some land. I'd hate to see us all end up on concrete someday.'

■■■■■■■■■■

At the rate African Americans are losing land, city life seems predestined. Nationally, nearly one of four black-owned farms was forced out of business during the 1980s, according to figures compiled by the Texas Department of Agriculture. Between 1982 and 1987 the rate of attrition was 3.6 times that among white farmers.

In 1982, the U.S. Civil Rights Commission reported that minority applicants were more than twice as likely as white applicants to be denied loans by the federal Farmers Home Administration. If the trend continued, the agency cautioned, African-

American farmers would disappear by the century's end. In 1990, 14 percent of minority farmers were receiving direct government loans, compared to 34 percent of whites.

Until Mike Espy was elected to Congress in 1986, black farmers' troubles received relatively little public attention. Because all small farmers were struggling, the African-American farm crisis was largely overlooked. Mr. Espy, a Democrat who is Mississippi's first black congressman since Reconstruction, had hardly unpacked when he began loudly lamenting the plight of African-American farmers.

His efforts resulted in a 1990 bill that provides outreach services and technical assistance for minority and disadvantaged farmers and ranchers. Still, it will take time to resolve the problems.

Mr. Kitchen knows several African-American farmers who hastened their own demise with poor record-keeping and unsophisticated management. Thousands have failed to keep up with taxes or to provide for maintenance after their deaths.

Others were victimized by opportunists, says Don Albrecht, a Texas A&M University professor of rural sociology. Illiterate rural blacks who misunderstood contracts inadvertently signed away property rights.

Alarmed agricultural activists have hosted seminars in towns from the Virginia Tidewater to the Mississippi Delta and through the plains of Texas, says Charles Radford, a Smith County extension agent. They hope information — about financing and technical advances — will save farms and educate the public.

Says Mr. Radford: "You're seeing a last-ditch survival effort." In Texas, black farmers are holding their own — barely. In 1990, the state had 3,211 African-American farmers, more than any other state. Since 1982, their number has increased by 145.

■ A family legacy

There's a legacy here that few African Americans can claim: Oquince Edwards works the land his grandmother bought in 1881 in the Jackson community, 15 miles east of Tyler, Texas. His father planted the rows of loblolly pines that snake through his 540-acre farm.

He sells his sweet potatoes and watermelons to neighbors — people who can't pay prices posted at the local grocery store. "People around here can't afford going to Brookshire (supermarket)," Mr. Edwards says. "We give 'em a pretty good bargain."

James Alford, a Smith County extension agent, says it's typical of black farmers to sell on a limited scale. When banks and government loan programs deny operating funds, he says, the farmers can't produce enough for mass markets. Accustomed to rejection, they traditionally farm for food instead of profit and fail to develop long-term business plans.

"The amount of property those Edwardses have is remarkable for a black farmer anywhere," Mr. Alford says. "I wonder where Oquince would be if he'd been able to get adequate funds."

With farm work, the volunteer fire department and church meetings, Mr. Edwards is too busy to ponder past possibilities.

His days begin before sunrise and end after dark. The work invigorates Mr. Edwards. His clear brown skin and energetic pace reveal no traces of age. At 68, he leaps out of a truck and dashes down a row of sweet potatoes faster than a pair of 30-year-olds trying to follow him.

'I don't worry about his cows, and he don't worry about mine. We build his fence one day and fix mine the next.'

■ ■ ■ ■ ■ ■ ■ ■ ■ ■

His farm is a one-man operation. But he and his brother, Charles, who jointly own 140 of the 540 acres, work together on any task that requires more than one person. They also share much of their energy, equipment and enterprise with the Willis brothers, who own an adjoining farm.

"I don't worry about his cows, and he don't worry about mine," Oquince Edwards says. "We build his fence one day and fix mine the next. When you don't have money, it pays to have friends. We don't hardly get up, go to bed or go to church without one of us knowing where the other is."

These days, he contemplates the fortunes of other neighbors and thinks about his own future.

"All the land back there belonged to black folk," says Mr. Edwards, waving his arm expansively. "Old man Pearl died four years ago. The Internal Revenue Service took the place. I got cousins about to lose their land."

He scoops up a fistful of soft soil and lets it run through his fingers. His voice is sad: "This is sandy loam. It's good for potatoes and real sweet melons. The good Lord made this soil."

The young people who grew up here don't appreciate fine soil or farm life, Mr. Edwards says. Few live in this primarily black farming community. When black farmers Mr. Edwards' age and older die, many leave their property to heirs who have moved to the city.

"The youngsters, they sell everything," he says. "You can go down any road and see oil wells on top of what used to be black people's property."

His own children show no interest in farming. His daughter and son left the farm and rarely return. He's determined to keep his grandmother's land in the family, and he hopes his grandchildren like the land better than their parents do.

Mr. Edwards survived the invasion of Normandy and the Battle of the Bulge. He believes he'll win this war, too. "There's never been a nickel worth of mortgage on that farm, and there never will be," he says. "I'm crying, crying every day that, when I die, this ain't through."

▪ Dirt poor

Wrinkles crease the 48-year-old hand that grips a shiny metal walker. Albert Beall, the man propped against the walker, stands in the shade, watching a woman pull up purple-top and turnip greens that sprout from a quarter-acre field near the town of Lakeport, six miles east of Longview, Texas.

If he could, he would be beside the woman, his wife, Frankie.

But a recent back operation and hip-replacement surgery make crouching impossible. After 24 years of farming, all he can do is watch. "Farming's all I know," Mr. Beall says. "Don't think I'd work on another job. Out here, you're your own boss."

The morning dew makes the green leaves glisten. Summer was good to the vegetables, and they're healthier than the man who planted them. In fact, the tiny crop is the healthiest Mr. Beall has grown in years.

"We've had three bad years in a row," he says. "The weather cut our yield in half. Some years we got no yield. In farming, every year is different."

Warmth and water. Too much of either can kill a farm, Mr. Beall says. So can a lack of money.

The Bealls say they don't resent the floods or the droughts. What really tries their nerves is dealing with the federal Farmers Home Administration.

"The FmHA is hard on minority people," Mr. Beall says. Bob Hopper, chief of farmer programs for the FmHA in Texas, says the agency does not discriminate. He says privacy law prevents him from speaking about Mr. Beall's case, but Mr. Hopper points to federally mandated assistance to minority and socially disadvantaged farmers.

"We have an outreach program," Mr. Hopper says. "We have money specifically for land purchase. We make every effort we can to help all farmers, including African Americans."

Leroy Biggers, director of the Texas Department of Agriculture district office in Tyler, says the problems originate in the local FmHA committees. Farmers and representatives from local agricultural businesses sit on the committees. Historically, he says, members have been white.

"They determine the eligibility of applicants," Mr. Biggers says. "Who is to say local committees don't have prejudice?"

Mr. Hopper says the federal agency has increased efforts to diversify the racial composition of its county committees. Law requires that two committee members be elected and one appointed. "At this time, there are a number of black and Hispanic farmers on our committees," Mr. Hopper says. He says he cannot provide figures.

Mr. Beall describes the same runaround reported by other African-American farmers in recent congressional hearings. He says he received a small loan from the agency once. The money enabled him to plant 300 acres and gross between $18,000 and $20,000 for that year. But since then, he says, each time he has applied for a loan, he has been given additional forms to take home and fill out. When he returned the form, he was given another. And another. As planting time approached, he didn't have money for seed and fertilizer. After planting time passed, he was told that his loan had been approved, but that the local lending committee had run out of funds.

Mr. Hopper says that the lengthy loan process requires a lot of forms. He says it "involves all applicants regardless of their race. At times, it seems as though the paper never ends."

"Regulations are constantly changing," Mr. Hopper says. "When rules change, that creates more paperwork. It's a common complaint from all of our applicants."

"I think they want to see how much pressure they could put on me to run me out of farming," Mr. Beall says.

But he says he'll keep on farming. When commercial banks stopped giving him loans, he simply planted fewer acres. Now he figures the FmHA might come through with a loan if he proposes to plant only 35 acres.

"I can't be the type to let the down years get me down," Mr. Beall says. "If I do, I'm not a real farmer."

▪ A return to the land

At night, Timmothy Caldwell earns a living. During the day, he lives.

From 1976 to 1983, Mr. Caldwell would drive his truck into the woods near Red Springs, 14 miles northeast of Tyler. He parked on the edge of a 20-acre field and daydreamed. At night, as he worked on a tire factory's assembly line, memories of budding beans and baby chicks pushed aside the work at hand. In the day, the scent of turned earth crept into his sleep.

Mr. Caldwell's childhood paralleled that of lots of other

African-Americans raised in East Texas. He and his 15 siblings grew up on a dirt farm that supplied most of the family's food. They learned agriculture at school, and they practiced it at home.

When cotton ripened, everybody picked. No exceptions. As soon as they could, the Caldwell kids ran toward time clocks, regular pay and all the accompanying benefits. Timmothy, now 38, ran with the rest of them.

"I never was really interested in farming until I left," Mr. Caldwell says. "Then I moved to town and got bored. I had a lot of time on my hands."

Tyler, with all its charm, never offered the serenity of the countryside. Eventually, Mr. Caldwell and his dreams found themselves face to face with Smith County agricultural extension agents. "I'd go up to the office to get brochures on everything," Mr. Caldwell says. "I would stop in and talk to the people."

The meetings led to an unusual partnership, an agreement that permits Mr. Caldwell to fulfill most of his fantasies.

He farms the 20 acres during the day and builds tires at night. Cattle and catfish. Corn and onions. Potatoes, peas, peaches, peanuts, grapes, greens, squash, tomatoes, hay and a handful of other crops cover the once-wild property. The variety is rare among modern farms. It is rarer still among African-American farmers.

"If you'd seen it a few years ago," says Mr. Caldwell, "it didn't resemble this at all."

'I never was really interested in farming until I left (the farm).'

■ ■ ■ ■ ■ ■ ■ ■ ■ ■ ■

Experts from Prairie View A&M University's agricultural extension service provide information and technical help. They encourage the diversity found on the Caldwell farm, says Joe Radford, a Smith County extension agent. Mr. Caldwell's place is the only whole-farm demonstration project in Texas. He is being advised and monitored in an experimental program designed to boost profits among minority farmers and others with limited resources.

"I'm looking to break even or turn a profit this year," Mr. Caldwell says. "If you figure our grocery bill, we've never had a loss. Seventy-five percent of what we eat, we produce.

"For the past couple of years, they (the experts) have provided a lot of my seeds," Mr. Caldwell says. "They also input a lot of information. I had a lot of farming knowledge, but it was old-fashioned knowledge I got from watching my father."

By combining that old-fashioned knowledge with contemporary scientific techniques, Mr. Caldwell has achieved what many critics of family farming say is impossible. His success, limited though it is, suggests that a small property can be self-supporting and even profitable in this era of agricultural giants.

After eight- and sometimes 12-hour shifts at the tire factory, Mr. Caldwell rushes right home. Today he cranks up his tractor engine before the engine of his car cools.

He mixes fertilizer with forage seed. Then, accompanied by Mr. Radford and a small herd of cows, he heads toward the pond with a pail of catfish food. As the fish begin to nibble, he softly asks Mr. Radford if he'll need to switch to a sinking feed if the water freezes. No, Mr. Radford explains, the fish might have difficulty eating if the food gets stuck in mud at the bottom.

After his physical exertions, the young farmer sits down at a kitchen counter for a round of mental exercise. With a yellow No. 2 pencil or a ball-point pen, he records every action in a detailed diary and jots down relevant questions and observations. The volume provides information for frequent consultations with agriculture experts. It also gives him invaluable problem-solving clues.

Last year, his tomatoes came up beautifully, then died before ripening. Flipping through the diary, he was reminded that he'd planted corn there before. The corn, he found, had depleted nitrogen needed by the tomatoes.

Mr. Caldwell says he's learned quite a bit more since then, and he's proud of his considerable knowledge.

"The average person sees this as hard, hot, sweaty work," he says. "It is. But to me, there's some glory to it."

November 25, 1990

SECTION III

·

HIDDEN TREASURES

·········

Hair-Raising Adventures

■■■■■■■■■■

I was game for a change, and I figured new hair would cost less than a new wardrobe.

When I was a little girl, my style was part-down-the-middle with two stiff pigtails (four or more if you had thick hair or hardly any). But I longed for curly ringlets. My aunt, who obliged most of my wishes, would press (hot comb) my hair with tons of Dixie Peach Pomade, then twist sections into fat rigatoni with a stovetop curling iron.

The ringlets would last for two, maybe three days. The ear and scalp burns would last longer.

A colleague who frequently changes her hairstyle walked in one day with a mass of wild ringlets. I wanted hair like hers. She confided it was a weave. I still wanted hair like hers.

She sent me to Traci Rhea, a Dallas hairdresser who specializes in the "latch lock" method of weaving. The process creates styles suited to business and professional women.

I was interested because I have a head full of hair and can't use chemical relaxers to straighten it. And my allergies to chemicals are compounded by another sensitivity: Black hairdressers say I'm tender-headed, a condition that accounts for the involuntary wincing and flinching that begins as soon as I see a comb.

In New York where I attended college, I wore my hair as short as my eyebrows. There were barbers aplenty who would near-shave my hair and give it a fashionable flair.

I wanted hair like hers. She confided it was a weave. I still wanted hair like hers.

■■■■■■■■■■

Because of my demanding schedule, the promise of a carefree 'do — latch-lock curls require very little maintenance — is the bait that lured me to Traci's shop.

■

I arrive slightly jittery. Will anyone be able to tell the curls aren't real? Will I look like me? Will I be here all night?

The supplies look more suited for a quilting bee than a weave. Among the wares is a narrow spool of black thread, a curved needle, a rug latch hook. Two bags of dark brown curls stand ready on a nearby stool.

Traci combs out my hair, then parts a quarter-inch section from the temple to the nape of my neck. She quickly cornrows (the reverse of French-braiding) the section flat against my scalp and repeats this until my crown is covered with long rows of braids.

Because my hair is shoulder length and the ends hang beneath the hairline, she braids the loose ends together and sews them flat.

The next step floors me: She takes curly, wide strands of synthetic hair and loops them around the tip of the rug hook. Starting at my neck, she pokes the latch hook into the cornrow and pulls the curl through. Thus threaded, she knots the divided strand.

"Applying the hair strand by strand gives you fullness," she explains.

Traci repeats the process for the next two hours, covering my head in shiny ringlets.

■

Traci, a Detroit native, says the latch lock is a method similar to one used in her hometown.

"In Detroit, a woman cornrowed my hair, then pulled human strands through with a crochet hook," 26-year-old Traci recalls. "It didn't stay. It was embarrassing. Locks slipped out every day until finally, I took it all out.

"I liked the idea, but I wanted something secure so my clients wouldn't have to worry about pieces falling out."

James Harris, owner of New York Salon in Manhattan, says Traci's technique is similar to that used by custom wig makers. Some New York stylists practice interlocking, a weave technique that involves hooking extension hair on with a crochet needle as the client's hair is braided. Mr. Harris, known for styling *Essence* magazine models and stars such as Diana Ross and Patti LaBelle, says that because interlocking takes between eight and 12 hours, it is expensive.

"It has its market, but it's a small market," he says.

Traci uses different tools and the amount of time is smaller.

The procedure, at $162, may strain some pocketbooks. But many black women chemically straighten their hair every six to eight weeks, then shell out between $20 and $35 a week for a shampoo and set. By comparison, Traci says, latch locks, available in straight, kinky or curly styles, are a bargain. The curly locks last at least two months before the process has to be repeated.

The curly locks last at least two months before the process has to be repeated.

■ ■ ■ ■ ■ ■ ■ ■ ■ ■

The cost is also less than that of traditional interlocked weaves, which can range from $500 to $1,000, says Mr. Harris, of New York Salon.

Since Ms. Rhea introduced latch locks to Dallas a year ago, 50 women have chosen the new procedure. Most, Ms. Rhea says, have been professional women who want the convenience of braids, but whose careers required a more conventional look.

Childhood fantasies aside, after two years of braids, I wanted something different. At a conference we attended in Kansas City, strangers kept approaching my co-worker who wears the latch locks. The comments were complimentary. No one had seen the style before and every woman wanted it.

I have it and I'm happy.

September 18, 1991

Table for One

■ ■ ■ ■ ■ ■ ■ ■ ■ ■

he crunch of a knife cutting through celery is the only sound in this tiny Dallas restaurant. There are no bussers banging pans, no waiters yelling orders, no executive chefs barking commands at line cooks.

At the Dining Table, there is no hierarchy and little help. Just Cassondra Armstrong — chef, waitress, shopper, cashier, dishwasher and dreamer. Some days, eating a meal at her restaurant is a lot like dropping by your aunt's house for lunch. A phone hangs from her ear as she greets customers. Or she'll bring her plate out and join you for breakfast. Other days, when each table is crowded with hungry diners and she's running between the kitchen and the dining room in her white Avias, the restaurant seems like something out of a skit from *Saturday Night Live*.

The five-table restaurant is tucked in Elmwood, a neighborhood of post-war bungalows and ranch-style houses.

The inside looks like a 1950s diner. Instead of jukeboxes, though, you'll find a vase of fresh flowers on each table. One of her few indulgences, Ms. Armstrong has bunches of gladiolas, azaleas and alstroemerias delivered every few days. The roses come from her own garden. Her medals, a silver from the 1991 Sysco culinary salon and a bronze from the 1990 Texas Chef's Association culinary salon hang behind the cash register. Floral print fabric covers the table tops. Framed photos of the chef's prettiest dishes adorn the white walls. There's a swirl of smoked salmon in one picture, a tray of carved mango, sliced strawberries and scalloped cantaloupe in another. Photos of crystal dishes brimming with green pesto, chilled asparagus and mounds of perfect salade nicoise hang on another wall.

The award-winning chef starts out slowly this morning. Last night she decided the day's special's — roast beef, roast chicken and pasta primavera — but this morning she needs to stock up for the next few days. She jots items to buy on a yellow legal pad, and leans down to tie her sneakers. She needs both.

She is headed to Sam's Wholesale Club, about 20 minutes behind schedule. Items and aisles are etched somewhere in her memory. In less than 30 minutes, she tosses Styrofoam trays, Italian sausage, prime rib, chicken breasts, turkey pastrami, croissants, tomatoes, baby carrots, broccoli and cauliflower into an oversized cart.

She stocks up at Sam's once a week. Most mornings she stops by Rhoton's Food for Less, a neighborhood grocery store.

"I try not to drive north," she says. "It takes too much time."

Ms. Armstrong checks her watch. She wants to cruise past a house on 12th Street. At least once a week, she drives by this two-story Victorian. The Dining Table celebrates its first birthday this month, and already she's planning its graduation. "God willing," she'll find money to buy the house and convert it into the kind of restaurant she reads about in gourmet magazines.

'I've always wanted to be the first black woman to own a four-star restaurant in Dallas.'

■ ■ ■ ■ ■ ■ ■ ■ ■ ■

"I've always wanted to be the first black woman to own a four-star restaurant in Dallas," she says.

Back at the Dining Table, she arranges her vases and begins chopping vegetables and slicing fruit.

"I'm a taster," she says, dipping a tasting spoon into a bowl of pasta salad. "Needs more onion?"

She stirs up a pitcher of lemonade, then checks the chicken, which has been roasting slowly. Next, she whips up a bowl of eggless potato salad.

"A lot of my lunch customers are older," Ms. Armstrong says. "They probably need to watch their cholesterol. Besides, eggs cost too much."

Ms. Armstrong's grandmother, Helen "Granddear" Brooks is helping out today. She's lending a hand because her granddaughter recently had minor surgery and is supposed to be taking it easy.

"I don't want her trying to do too much," Mrs. Brooks says. "She's always got so much to do."

Mrs. Brooks says she sometimes wonders why in the world her granddaughter has chosen such hard work.

"She's not making a whole lot of money," Mrs. Brooks says. "I worry. Some days, as many as 15 or 20 people come in. Some days just four or five. Cassondra has a B.S. in business and I wonder why she didn't go into that. She's a trouper, though, and she's really happy with what she's doing."

Ms. Armstrong says she's looking to make a profit, not a killing, and she accepts the financial challenges as a matter of course.

> **'You don't go into this business to make money. You go into it because you like people.'**
>
> ■ ■ ■ ■ ■ ■ ■ ■ ■ ■

"I'm poor," she says matter-of-factly. "You don't go into this business to make money. You go into it because you like people."

Besides, says Ms. Armstrong, she gave corporate culture a shot following her 1983 graduation from Dallas Baptist University. She worked in sales at Neiman-Marcus and briefly as a chef apprentice at the Hyatt Regency after completing culinary school at El Centro Community College in 1991.

"Everything was hard, hot or heavy," she says of her apprenticeship. "Your opinion doesn't matter. It was very frustrating."

What she learned, she says, was that the corporate climb is very long and not always satisfying. She also found that she preferred bossing herself to being bossed.

She started a catering business in her parent's kitchen in 1986. Today it helps float the restaurant when customers don't materialize.

"The restaurant is kind of creepy-crawling," Ms. Armstrong says. "The catering is probably 80 percent of my income."

People who visit the restaurant discover it by accident or by word of mouth — her mouth. Ms. Armstrong says she can't afford more traditional print advertising. Michael T. Caesar, an advertising salesman for *Dallas Weekly*, met the chef when she catered his newspaper's Christmas party last year. He tried the Dining Table, and now makes the nine-mile drive from his South Dallas office two or three times a week.

"I don't like mushy, cooked-down vegetables that have had all the nutrients cooked out," Mr. Caesar says. "Her vegetables are always nice and crisp, full of fiber. Being 40 I'm concerned with how long I'm going to live."

Ms. Armstrong remembers always having this intense "thing" for food. When her now-retired grandmother, Mrs. Brooks, prepared soups and other goodies for the Dallas Museum of Art, young Cassondra begged to tag along.

"She always asked if she could work," Mrs. Brooks says. "When Lady Bird (Johnson) came, she met everyone in the kitchen, including Cassondra. When Jimmy Carter came, she had her picture taken with him."

Ms. Armstrong says parties organized by caterers in North Dallas left her starry-eyed. Her grandmother moonlighted for these caterers, and Cassondra usually begged to go.

"They had fabulous parties," Ms. Armstrong recalls. "There were always lots and lots of fresh flowers. Lots of silver and crystal. The food was so festive. It was almost like a fairy tale."

The caterers hired Cassondra even though she was underage. She copied their names and phone numbers off her paychecks. That list, and names from her Neiman-Marcus client book, provided contacts for the catering company she eventually started.

A gospel radio sticker is pasted on the rear bumper of Ms. Armstrong's maroon Chevy Lumina. A devout Christian, she believes in divine intervention. The day she gave the Hyatt a three-week notice, a friend phoned to tell her the little restaurant on Ferndale was available for rent.

"The Lord was looking out for me," Ms. Armstrong says. "I'd been thinking about whether I was ready to step out on faith and do it."

God gave her another sign, she says. Family friends had just moved their day-care center to a new location, leaving them with a bumper crop of institutional-size kitchen appliances. Ms. Armstrong bought the equipment and brought the restaurant up to code with the $2,000 nest egg she'd been saving for the right opportunity.

"There were 21 code violations," she recalls. "The people here before had done some 'Southern' engineering and it wouldn't pass inspection. I had to replace a wall and redo the plumbing. Every penny was gone before I could turn on the electricity and water. But I'm a believer. I just sat here and read my Bible."

Ann Marsh, the hairdresser from the salon around the corner, is the entire morning breakfast rush. She asks to have an order of carry-out bacon, eggs and toast delivered.

'She never slaps it together and she never complains.'

■ ■ ■ ■ ■ ■ ■ ■ ■ ■

"You can hardly go anywhere and find this kind of food," Mrs. Marsh says. "She makes you feel like you're sitting up in the Mansion (a chic Dallas restaurant). She never slaps it together and she never complains."

But Ms. Armstrong is wrinkling her brow at Mrs. Marsh's breakfast.

"Garnish," she mutters. "This needs garnish."

Mrs. Brooks peers over her granddaughter's shoulder as she transforms the Styrofoam tray into a *Gourmet* magazine spread of eggs, bacon and toast nestled in a colorful ring of yellow cantaloupe, curly green lettuce and red and yellow marigolds.

"I'm not artistic," says Mrs. Brooks, sighing. "I can't fix it pretty like she does. She's a perfectionist."

The hustle and bustle, the watching her granddaughter work, has worn out Mrs. Brooks.

"This is taking its toll on Granddear," Mrs. Brooks says. "I could easily be home reading the paper and looking at *Wheel of Fortune*. But with your children, you want to be out there and be supportive."

An hour before lunch, Ms. Armstrong slips out the side door

and heads for her herb garden. She squats and tears tiny bunches of rosemary, basil, Italian parsley and bright bell peppers. She waves the aromatic bouquet beneath her nose and inhales.

"You know," she says, smiling, "I've always wanted to be the black Martha Stewart."

September 15, 1992

Calvin Strong and Tall

▪ ▪ ▪ ▪ ▪ ▪ ▪ ▪ ▪ ▪

O n a typical weekend night, it seems as if 8 million passers-by stop to talk to Calvin Lane.

Well, 8 million might be stretching it, but just a little.

A recent Saturday night: At least 100 pedestrians pause when they spot Calvin — bon vivant, automobile recovery specialist (read: repo man) and most noticeably, 7-foot-4-inch doorman at Sambuca, the trendiest of trendy eateries in the downtown Dallas bistro area, Deep Ellum.

The timid ones gawk. The bold ones talk. Some of the ones in cars brake to a screeching halt.

A white stretch limousine circles the busy block. Each time the car approaches the Elm Street restaurant, there is the tiny whir of an electric motor as one window slides down. A head of fluffy white hair pops into view. Then the window glides up. The third time, a little old lady wearing a red-knit pantsuit emerges.

"I just had to shake your hand, young fella," she says. "You are a sight. I'm five-one. In all my 78 years I've never seen anyone as beautiful as you."

Before Calvin can introduce himself, she slips back into the limousine.

Calvin takes it in stride.

He takes everything in stride. The man who stops and lifts his black T-shirt to proudly show Calvin his freshly pierced navel. The parading female exhibitionist dressed in a complicated bondage shirt and a see-through girdle — sans panties — who says hello each time she passes.

Sambuca's management takes advantage of Calvin's good nature. The menu reads: "Sambuca respectfully requests no cigar or pipe smoking or Calvin will have a talk with you."

Strangers walk up to Calvin and ask to measure their hands next to his. He says yes. Others ask to pose next to him for photos.

"I go blind sometimes, people take so many pictures," Calvin says. "I've posed for over 100 pictures in a weekend."

Many swear he's a professional basketball player. A woman who smells like wine insists, "You're (former Dallas Mavericks player) Roy Tarpley, right? I've seen you on the news."

Two minutes later, a man is asking him, "You play for the Mavs, right?"

"No," Calvin answers.

"You lyin', man?" the man persists.

If Calvin did play professional basketball, he'd be one of the National Basketball Association's four tallest hoopsters. Only Manute Bol, at 7-foot-7, would hover higher.

Lechia Hargrove, Calvin's longtime girlfriend, fell in love with her fella when he lumbered into her place of business: Frank's King Size Clothes. She liked his good nature, but barely noticed his height.

"I worked with a man who is seven-one," Ms. Hargrove explains. "All sizes come in here."

But when they're out in public together, strangers make her aware of his height — in sometimes unwelcome ways.

"I get mad," she says. "When you're having a romantic evening, people walk up to the table and say, 'Who do you play for?' They've practically turned our tables over."

The interruptions and constant inquiries mostly amuse Calvin, Ms. Hargrove says.

"Really," she says. "It doesn't bother him. He'll always take the few seconds to say, 'I'm seven-four.' He tells kids, 'If you eat your greens, you'll be like me.'"

Ms. Hargrove, 26, likens the attention to the compliments lavished on drop-dead-beautiful women and sexy men.

"It's like someone saying, 'Ooh, you're beautiful,'" Ms. Hargrove says. "Same thing with Calvin. He likes his height. It makes him stand out."

November 15, 1991

Cuttin' Heads

■ ■ ■ ■ ■ ■ ■ ■ ■ ■

R esign yourself to a timeless wait. That's what you'll do at Sessions Barber and Beauty Shop.

While patrons wait, they talk. They talk about a riot at Fair Park during the late 1960s. "The police let loose these German shepherds," says customer Allan Evans. He shadowboxes to illustrate his story, and everyone cracks up. "This man fought that dog like a natural man."

Customers talk about the melee during a recent basketball game between two North Carolina colleges. They talk about Social Security. Men talk about women. Women talk about men. Everyone talks about relationships, says Mr. Evans, a 15-year Sessions patron.

"We've developed a rapport in here," explains Mr. Evans, a devilish chuckle creeping into his voice. "We can pick up all the local gossip — who shot who, whose old lady left home."

Afros and other styles have come and gone and come again, but Sessions — with all that good talk — has stayed at the intersection of Navaro and Toronto streets, beautifying West Dallas heads for 26 years.

Don't be alarmed if a man rushes to your car as you're squeezing into a space in front of Sessions. He wants to wash your windows, but he'll shrug and disappear if you don't accept the offer.

Some people might find Sessions' cast of characters intimidating. There's Shirley, the neighborhood Greek chorus, who regularly makes grand entrances. She trips over customers' legs, then rants, raves and cusses about drug dealers, death, decay and destruction. Then there's Don, a timid man, a fixture as sure as the hair clippings that coat the floor. He ducks through the shop and waits to be asked to sweep or perform some other chore.

Only snotty people aren't welcome at Sessions, says Marian

Brown, a stylist at the storefront salon.

"Other places, I'd be around a lot of stuffed shirts," Ms. Brown says. "I don't like to deal with stuck-up people, period."

Merciless teasing is the preferred form of communication. An older man becomes a target when he takes off a gimme cap to reveal a big bush of gray hair.

"If I try to cut your hair with my scissors," says barber James Hamilton, "I'll end up with arthritis. I know a good pet shop in Oak Cliff that has heavy-duty clippers...."

What you get is what you see. The teal and pink walls are more Miami than Dallas, but who cares? Hot pink hides dirt real well, says Opal Sessions, the 60-ish owner of the cinder-block building.

"They've been nice colors," says Mrs. Sessions, "not something that have wore me out."

Combs and brushes bounce around in glass jars of green sterilizing solution. Barbers use a tattered spiral notebook to jot down "appointments" rarely adhered to. Wide bands of electrical tape on the red Naugahyde-and-velvet chairs patch the splits and cracks left by thousands of black and brown backsides.

Money isn't squandered on printed posters. Handwritten signs tell customers to limit phone calls to three minutes. They list prices and inform customers that cuts cost a dollar extra after 10 p.m. The signs don't tell that the directive was scrawled in a futile attempt to discourage patrons from plopping into a chair at 9:59 p.m.

'If I try to cut your hair with my scissors, I'll end up with arthritis. I know a good pet shop over in Oak Cliff that has heavy-duty clippers... '

The close quarters at Sessions leave no space for a stove, hot plate or microwave. But that doesn't stop beauticians and barbers from eating hot meals. They merely heat up containers of food in the hood of a hair dryer.

With slight modifications, the hairdos of yesteryear appear on the head of every other person who walks out of Sessions.

"A lot of the cuts I give now, the kids think is something new," says Mr. Hamilton, shaking hair from a customer's bib the way a matador waves a cape. "But the fade was the standard haircut when I first started."

Retro 'dos are standard for women, too. Eula Holyfield, one of stylist Loleta Cotton's longtime customers, sports the scalp-hugging finger waves popular during the Harlem Renaissance of the 1920s. Buckets of relaxer and a half-dozen crimpers and curlers rest in a corner. They await scores of customers who abandoned straight styles during the natural-loving '60s and '70s.

At Sessions, women in nurse's uniforms or sweatsuits sit next to tiny girls in threadbare dresses and men in business suits or worn overalls.

Buckets of relaxers and a half-dozen crimpers and curlers sit in a corner.
▪ ▪ ▪ ▪ ▪ ▪ ▪ ▪ ▪ ▪

"Doctors, lawyers, preachers, teachers — it don't matter," Ms. Cotton says. "Like they say at church, 'Come as you are.'"

Customers come from Dallas suburbs as far as 10 and 15 miles away for the hairstyles and easygoing atmosphere.

"When I go out of town, I wait till I get back for a haircut," says Charles Williams, an engineer from the Dallas suburb of Arlington. "Sometimes I go for six weeks at a time."

Despite pleas from family and friends who urge him to find another hair salon in what they consider a safer area, Mr. Williams fixes himself in a Sessions chair at 7:30 each Friday night.

"My mom says, 'Boy, don't go over there,'" Mr. Williams says. "People say, 'Where do you get your hair cut?' I say, 'West Dallas.' They say, 'West Dallas?'"

Stylists face the same disbelief when they meet potential clients or colleagues who want to know where they do business.

"In beauty school," says Ms. Brown, "everyone was afraid of West Dallas."

But patrons at Sessions say the fears are unfounded. Everybody in West Dallas seems to know the shop and feel at home there. The mutual respect might be measured by the fact that it never has been a target of crime.

The neighborhood is also an economical place to cut hair.

"If you talk about renting a building in North Dallas and a building in West Dallas, there's a whole lot of difference," Mr. Hamilton says.

No one at Sessions is getting rich off the work. The cost for women's hairdos varies because of the variety of styles and chemical processes requested, but barbers charge $6 for haircuts. Neighborhood residents can afford those prices.

"If you get your prices up and don't be busy, you won't make as much money as you do if you keep the prices down," Mr. Hamilton says. "I found out a long time ago that I can't make as much money as I need."

Monday evenings — "family night" — Mr. Hamilton and others donate their talents to the heads of their own families and neighborhood kids whose families can't spare the money for a trip to a salon. An unending line of frightened-faced children waited for trims one recent Monday.

"I enjoy the work," Mr. Hamilton says. "If you are in a business and don't enjoy it, it makes your life hard."

Although Mr. Hamilton longs for the days when he can spend fewer hours on his feet, he has no plans to move.

"Once you stay in a place so long, it's not easy to leave," he says. "Sometime people come through who haven't been here for 10 to 15 years. They want to see if we're still here. What would they do if we weren't?"

January 27, 1990

Pier Group

■ ■ ■ ■ ■ ■ ■ ■ ■ ■

J ust as Richard Taylor puffs up and begins to brag about fishing away the next 48 hours, Alice Taylor arrives to correct her husband's notion.

"Hey, Punkin," Mr. Taylor says.

Mrs. Taylor barely nods to acknowledge the greeting.

"When you plan on comin' home?" she asks.

It's sunset and Richard, 54, has been at the pier long enough to see another sunset and one sunrise. A cooler filled with buffalo, striped bass, crappie and catfish are the fruits of this truck driver's labor.

Alice couldn't care less. Life in south Dallas County gets lonesome without her man, who, she says, is not even crazy about seafood.

"He hardly eats it," says Mrs. Taylor. "And I hate fish. He puts them in the freezer so long, it takes the taste out of them. Fishing to him is like gambling to somebody else. It's like he's got a fever."

They all have the fever, folks who drive out to the "pier," a partially submerged tar road that slopes into the little waves of Lake Ray Hubbard, a reservoir 10 miles east of Dallas. Rogers Callahan, 57, makes the trip from Dallas at least twice each week. The retired postal worker has passed a nearby abandoned bait, tackle and barbecue stand in rain, sleet and snow for almost 15 years.

"I love catching fish, but my wife, she gives them away," says Mr. Callahan. "I'd come down here whether I caught fish or not."

Why?

"For one thing, it's the anticipation of the strike," he says. "Another thing, you don't have to worry about snakes and the people are friendly."

James Brown easily could have been thinking about this place when he sang *A Man's, Man's, Man's World* back in '66. Women are welcome here and a few venture out, but they don't seem to take to the solitude and weather extremes the way guys do, says Willie Lawson, a scraggly blond who averages about 20 hours a week at the pier.

"Coming down here is a lonely type occupation," Mr. Lawson, 38, says. "The fish, they don't talk."

Men who come here don't pay mind to differences like race, age or class. Together they are an easy mix of black and white, red and brown. Cadillac and Pinto drivers sit side by side as do the young, the old and the middle-aged.

On hot days, fishermen here bare shirtless chests and protruding bellies to the sun. Those prone to heat exhaustion sling cold, wet towels over their heads pharaoh-style. Mr. Lawson also fills his gimme cap with chunks of ice for a little moist air conditioning.

"I'm trying to cool my temples down a little bit," says Mr. Lawson, a high-performance auto parts salesman.

To avoid several trips to their cars, the men haul their dozens of fishing rods, bait, tackle, snacks, insect repellent, gas lamps and flashlights in two-wheel wire baskets, faded red wagons and rusty wheelbarrows.

On the way to their perches, they nod silent hellos. Once where they want to be, the more experienced men screw 20 to 30 rods to the rails of the old bridge with 6-inch C-clamps. They unfold chairs, line up their lamps, then set radios at barely audible levels to talk shows, baseball games and country music stations.

Theirs is a fellowship of silence.

Together they are an easy mix of black and white, red and brown. Cadillac and Pinto drivers sit side by side.

"You got one?" is the question that most often cuts through the night air. Except for the whirring wings of mayflies and the crunch of gravel as they rush over to watch a battle between fish and fisherman, the splash of a surfacing fish and a bit of dialogue are the only sounds on the quiet pier.

"We got to concentrate," explains Comer Taylor, 68, a retired railroad worker. "We didn't come out here to conversate."

And while they concentrate, many of the men stoke themselves with cigarettes, sodas, beer and gut-burning combinations of salty, oily foods: tins of sardines, stacks of Saltines, cans of mackerel and jars of peanut butter.

Live minnows and dead shrimp hang from the curve of most bait hooks. But Lacy "Buffalo Man" Anderson uses a secret recipe that helps him catch baskets of fish and has earned him the respect of his pier colleagues. His namesake, the buffalo fish, he says, is especially drawn to the brown, piquant dough balls he rolls with flour, cotton-seed meal, anise and vanilla extracts.

Fishing is the quiet Christian therapy Lacy needs to continue his recovery from a cocaine and Jack Daniels addiction that cost him his job, home and family. He fishes like "all those boys in the Bible" to give food to hungry people who listen to his gentle proselytizing. He also fishes for old women who remind him of his deceased mother, a buffalo lover.

"Mamma used to say, "Go get me a buffalo, baby,"" says Lacy. "Then I'd run to the fish market."

And he fishes for sport.

"This is as close as you'll get to deep-sea fishin' without deep-sea fishin'," Lacy says. "I wrestled with one one day and he tore off with my rod and reel. One hundred dollars down the drain."

"What's so fun about it, you can't see them bite," he says. "They sneak up on you like thieves. Could be a whale down there."

October 17, 1989

A Good Name

■ ■ ■ ■ ■ ■ ■ ■ ■ ■

In case anyone wondered, Joe Blow isn't just a figure of speech. He lives in the North Dallas suburb of Addison and has spent a lifetime escaping the fuss over his handle.

"Aren't there any more Joe Blows?" he asks, a bit exasperated.

Not in the Dallas phone book.

For the record, Joseph Benjamin Blow is a junior. He attends church, makes mean barbecue and banana pudding, raises his three daughters, jogs a lot and looks for work.

He's thankful that Marshall, Texas, was the kind of hometown where being Joe Blow was no big deal. "I didn't hear any remarks until I got to college," Mr. Blow says. "I always thought of it as a good name."

A tall, elegant man who resembles jazz vocalist Bobby McFerrin, Mr. Blow dumped his identity albatross when he discovered women. He simply lied a lot during his dating days. Admiring women met John Cooper, Robert Cooper or Joe Cooper. Anybody but Joe Blow.

'Aren't there any more Joe Blows?'

■ ■ ■ ■ ■ ■ ■ ■ ■ ■

"My name was too easy to remember," he says. "If I had told every girl I tried to talk to, imagine the whiplash."

The sham caught up with him, usually while he was on the town with another woman. A previous date would greet him by the fake name five or six times before Joe Blow realized to whom she was speaking. That evening's date sat there perplexed, suspicious and wondering who had charmed her.

"It would be real embarrassing," he said. "But when you're out there lying and groping, you grab what's there."

Over the years, his name has subjected Mr. Blow, 41, to the kind of attention usually reserved for politicians, athletes or entertainers. At work, clients sought him out, saying, "All my life, I've wanted to meet Joe Blow." In Houston, his home phone received more than its share of calls from a disbelieving public that thought he had time to talk.

"None of them cursed me out or anything."

Callers were polite, familiar, curious, but never nasty.

"Is Joe Blow there?" they'd ask in a tone that suggested they'd known him all of their lives. In a soft-voiced, very East Texas twang, Mr. Blow told callers that he was the person they wanted. Without fail, they'd then ask, "Is this *the* Joe Blow?"

Calls came so frequently that the family changed its number a few times before reluctantly requesting that it be unlisted. A bashful Mr. Blow also developed little tricks to protect his privacy. Name tags at conferences never pose problems, for example. "Generally I put down J.B. Blow."

'I would never change it. I never wished it wasn't my name.'

■ ■ ■ ■ ■ ■ ■ ■ ■ ■

While he is job hunting, the former delivery service operations supervisor finds that pseudonyms are better than the real thing.

"If I make an appointment, generally I make it in another name."

After he inquired about one job, a receptionist at an employment agency asked for his phone number. But when he told her his name, she slammed the phone down in his ear.

"I called back. She was very unpleasant," Mr. Blow said. "I never bothered calling her back again."

Despite the difficulties of defending his name, Mr. Blow says he appreciates its uniqueness.

"I would never change it," he says. "I never wished it wasn't my name. If anything, I'd probably make use of it."

The surname Blow affects other members of the family, too. A suitor once accused Joe's sister Ruth of fibbing after she told him her full name.

"He said, 'I guess you have a brother named Joe Blow.'"

Ruth responded the only way she could.

"Yes," Ruth said. "As a matter of fact, I do."

With complete strangers tossing her father's name around so frequently, Mr. Blow's 13-year-old daughter Vantrese grew up believing her father was a star.

"The first day of school, in my theater arts class, the teacher talked about Joe Blow," says Vantrese. "I raised my hand and I said, 'That's my father.' Everybody looked at me."

Vantrese also likes the fact that her father's name often appears in print.

"My dad's famous," she says. "He's in books and everything."

But like Greta Garbo, Joe Blow would rather be left alone.

"I'm a very boring person."

August 7, 1989

BY THE BOOK

Alice in Wonderland

■ ■ ■ ■ ■ ■ ■ ■ ■ ■

BOONVILLE, Calif. — A series of two-lane mountain roads crisscrosses through the Anderson Valley, home to vineyards, country inns, apple orchards and Alice Walker. You won't happen by the writer's house. Perched on a steep hill, it sits high above a dirt road off the main highway, marked with a sign that says "private." From the very bottom of Ms. Walker's property, where a guest cottage nestles into a tree-shaded corner, the main house appears a vertical climb away. For the less fit, a weathered bench waits at the halfway mark. But the writer conquers the incline, a series of 45-degree switchbacks, without pausing, without sucking an extra breath. She trained for the climb, which she sometimes makes several times a day, in the red-clay hills of central Georgia. "When I was a girl, my mother was heavy," she says. "Real heavy, you know. One of my jobs was to push her up the hill." She giggles at the recollection and relays the events of her morning, spent alone, baking sweet potatoes and transferring geraniums to ornamental pots.

Ms. Walker, who is 48, cherishes busy-by-herself days like these. In the coming months, there won't be many. In a month, 175,000 copies of her newest novel, *Possessing the Secret of Joy*, will be in bookstores nationwide. Her publisher has persuaded her to go on an eight-city "educational" tour that will take her away from this hillside haven. *Possessing*, her fifth novel, ex-

The writer conquers the incline, a series of 45-degree switchbacks, without sucking an extra breath.

■ ■ ■ ■ ■ ■ ■ ■ ■ ■

amines female circumcision — a human-rights issue that has consumed her since she began writing the book.

"Because of the subject matter, it requires a kind of educational process," Ms. Walker says. "So many people have never heard of female genital mutilation.... That's why it's important to prepare people for it and also to appear in communities and talk to people about it."

To Ms. Walker, a self-described "womanist," clitorectomy is an extreme form of child abuse and patriarchal oppression — yet another way humans injure one another, hurt animals and scourge the earth. To her, the cosmos is interconnected.

"What I'm trying to do is help people understand that the world is one," she says. "It is completely integrated and whole as an ecosystem." Her voice fills with conviction; her hands move with the cadence of her speech. In her mind, clitorectomy deserves no less attention than, say, arms reduction. "I see the failure of so much healing being the inability to understand that there is no healing of the part without the healing of the whole," Ms. Walker says. "You cannot have a happy Europe and a miserable Africa. You cannot have a prosperous and posh Beverly Hills and have an impoverished south-central Los Angeles. It's not right. It's not balance. It's not healthy."

'What I'm trying to do is help people understand that the world is one.'

■ ■ ■ ■ ■ ■ ■ ■ ■ ■

This is the Alice Walker whom everyone imagines. The dreamer whose fictional universes pay equal respect to animals, plants and people of every racial, cultural, religious and sexual orientation. The Pulitzer Prize-winning writer who pens grim pictures of domestic violence. The contemporary seer who discusses the horrors of ritual teeth grinding and the pleasures of orgasmic sex in the same sentence. "I mean, you can only claim you have freedom of expression if you express yourself," Ms. Walker says. "I talk about my feet. I talk about my head. I talk about my hair, you know. I talk about my vulva. Why not? I want women to really affirm themselves and the magic of their bodies."

There is no one in American letters quite like Alice Walker, says University of Pennsylvania scholar Houston A. Baker Jr., director of the Center for the Study of Black Literature and Culture. "Walker's concerns may seem extreme, but they are as serious as anything we're likely to deal with," Dr. Baker says. "There are not nearly enough people who have enough talent who are coming forward and standing up the way Alice Walker is standing up. No matter how it's articulated, her concern is finally very serious."

The issues she tackles — spousal abuse, female circumcision, infidelity — are so serious that some assume that Ms. Walker is humorless and strident. Wrong, says Belvie Rooks, an old friend who helped Ms. Walker and writer-editor Robert Allen run a small publishing company during the mid-1980s.

"Because she takes on all these weighty things, people don't see the humor," Ms. Rooks says. "She is the funniest person I know. She'll have you rolling on the floor."

A case in point is the name of her Anderson Valley home. She christened it Temple Jook House. "Jook house" is the Gullah phrase for roadhouse. (Gullah is a kind of black speech from South Carolina and Georgia.) And "temple" — well, not exactly. The three words are carved in a wood shingle that hangs above the main gate. They sum up her view of home — a place for work, rest and play.

Ms. Walker says she throws a mean party. Complete freedom is encouraged behind the gate that protects Temple Jook House from the rest of the world. Kick off your shoes, if you'd like. If you don't mind frogs, strip off your clothes and dive into the chilly pond. Read on one of the porches or take a nap in the guest cottage. Just respect the residents — the foxes, the hawks, snakes, rabbits, spiders and hummingbirds — that rule this 40-acre spread.

Ms. Walker picked her house from a kit catalog. A group of "hippie builders" bolted it together and customized it to her specifications. Double doors fling open to welcome the aroma of eucalyptus. Windows on the west showcase the sun as it dips into the ocean, a 20-minute drive over the hills. When Ms. Walker isn't off to China, Jamaica or Georgia, she spends most of her time here. "It's as far west as I could go without falling into the Pacific," she says, laughing.

It's a world away from Eatonton, Ga., where she was born to Willie Lee Walker and Minnie Tallulah Grant Walker in 1944. The Walkers raised their eight children in a tiny house on a sharecropper's income. "We lived in very small houses that were really shacks, you know," Ms. Walker says. "We were very, very poor."

The relationship between sharecroppers and landowners — the modern manifestation of slavery, she says — continues to influence Ms. Walker's business dealings and personal finances. She mails her publisher completed manuscripts. She refuses cash advances, and she offers no prior glimpses, no proposals, no outlines. "I don't want to owe anybody anything," she says.

Leigh Haber, editor of *Possessing*, had just completed a promotional tour with Ms. Walker when she learned that a new book existed. "Alice had not described the novel to us," Ms. Haber says. "Nor did we know it was coming. I was on the phone with Alice on something else. She casually mentioned that she'd just completed a novel. My response to her telling me that there was a book was amazement. A few days later, I had the novel."

Editors at Harcourt Brace Jovanovich, Ms. Walker's publisher for 24 years, understand that a contract could restrict her sense of freedom, Ms. Haber says. Stifling Ms. Walker is the last thing they want to do.

"Anyone in fiction who sells more than 50,000 copies is considered a fairly successful writer," Ms. Haber says. Ms. Walker has penned five novels, two short-story collections, five volumes of poetry and two books of essays. Her fourth novel, *The Temple of My Familiar*, sold more than 200,000 copies. The best-selling *The Color Purple*, winner of the 1983 Pulitzer Prize for fiction, was made into a film by Steven Spielberg. It's a success story that stuns even Ms. Walker, who never intended to be a writer.

"You know," she says, "I just kind of found myself doing it. I remember wanting to be a scientist, wanting to be a pianist, wanting to be a painter. But all the while I was wanting to be these other things, I was writing. We were really poor, and writing was about the cheapest thing to do. You know, I feel amazed that I have been able to do exactly what I wanted to do."

She tires of talk and wanders out to a chair on the veranda, where she curls into a comfortable position. The movement reveals muscular upper arms and calves. "Yes," she murmurs. "I'm strong. I work very hard." Work might entail inspecting her waist-high irises, mulching a vegetable bed or picking a basket of strawberries, artichokes and collard greens. She recently mended the deer fences. She'll soon start clearing water weeds from the spring-fed pond to make room for swimming.

She moved here for the protected peace. The only voices raised here belong to the bullfrogs that protest her arrival at their pond's edge. "We'll be leaving soon," she tells them. They stop croaking.

Frida, a fluffy cat she named in honor of the late painter Frida Kahlo, keeps her company. She's far enough from friends to make dropping by an inconvenience. The silence, Ms. Walker says, is soothing. "I always longed to be an only child," she says. "I learned as a child that I could have peace only outdoors — away from my brothers, who were very much into being cowboys."

Ms. Walker writes in longhand in a three-room cabin halfway between the main house and the guest cottage. A recent earthquake shattered its windows and tilted the porch, but she doesn't mind. "Honey," she drawls, "it was only the earth moving."

Ms. Walker's speech — a mixture of sweet Georgia peach, Anderson Valley girl and Glinda the Good Witch — is startling in its softness, its careful modulation. She

She sounds more like a junior high school student than a world-famous writer.

■ ■ ■ ■ ■ ■ ■ ■ ■ ■

sounds more like a shy junior high school student than a world-famous writer — until she laughs, which she often does. "She has this deep-down-from-the-stomach laugh," says Ruth Walker Hood, an older sister. "It just fills me with joy."

Her serenity is deserved, Dr. Baker says. "I'm fairly non-reverential about writers," he says. "But Walker works very hard. She moves across genres. She tries a lot of different things.

"Creative-writing programs across the country are filled with bloated, fat white men making good money off the success of one

book," Dr. Baker adds. "One of the things Walker has done is survive and produce. That's not something African-American novelists
and poets have done very well."

Earnings from the movie version of *The Color Purple*, her books
and occasional speaking engagements afford Ms. Walker the kind of
indulgences she never imagined as a child. Her folk art collection in-
cludes intricately beaded Indian masks and pictures. Colorful
Afghan and antique Navajo rugs drape banisters and balconies.
Sculptures from Zimbabwe adorn outdoor tables. Open shelves
show off pottery and other decorative objects crafted by area artists.
Regal dining chairs, each upholstered with a unique Turkish rug,
surround a handmade table carved from dark brown wood.

There is a vast library, a San Francisco apartment, philanthropic
contributions and a Yale University educa-
tion for her only child, Rebecca Leventhal
Walker. All bought by a woman whose family was too poor to travel from Georgia to attend her graduation from Sarah Lawrence in
1965.

'Because I was always suicidal, I never expected to live past 30.'

■ ■ ■ ■ ■ ■ ■ ■ ■ ■

"Because I was always suicidal, I never expected to live past 30," Ms. Walker confides.
"My astonishment is that not only have I
lived to be older than 30, but that each year
has been better than the last, even consider-
ing all kinds of attacks, various struggles, political advances, setbacks and problems of
the world."

Survival and success have come with a price. Critics assailed her
depiction of spousal abuse in *The Color Purple* and, pointing to her
former marriage to Jewish lawyer Mel Leventhal, accused her of
having a vendetta against black men. Others have attacked her
themes and belittled her ability. "Of course, many of them were
completely frivolous in their criticism," she says.

Ruth Walker Hood, Ms. Walker's older sister, suspects that the
new novel will reignite the flames. "I said, 'Oh, Lord, poor Alice,'"
says Ms. Hood, who lives in Atlanta. "When *Possessing the Secret* hits
the market, she's going to take more heat than she did for *The Col-*

or Purple. But she's prepared this time."

In fact, she's downright upbeat. "I have really wonderful readers, you know," Ms. Walker says. "I have people who just are really with me — people who will really respond very well to this and who will be glad to use this book as a tool to help them study."

May 27, 1992

Ode to
Black Men

■ ■ ■ ■ ■ ■ ■ ■ ■ ■

ou've seen them on the evening news: handcuffed, spread-eagle, angry. You've seen them on the street corners. No money. No place to go. You've seen their women and children. Abandoned and poor.

These images of black men tell only part of their story, says poet Naomi Long Madgett. And the images, replayed on television and repeated in newspapers and novels, infuriate her. Driven by her rage, she vowed to show their unseen side. Her avenue: an anthology of poetry, *Adam of Ife: Black Women in Praise of Black Men*.

"I believe that, for every negative example of black manhood caught in the public spotlight, there are numerous others who are quietly living exemplary lives," Dr. Madgett writes in the introduction to the 235-page book. "Feeling a need to bring them out of the shadows and tell them, 'We see you; we know you are there, and we appreciate your presence in our lives,' I decided to pay tribute to them through poetry ...."

The book's theme presented a challenge to Dr. Madgett, a retired English professor who runs Lotus Press, the non-profit Detroit company that released it. Long before she solicited submissions, the editor and publisher says, she doubted she'd receive enough material for the anthology. Many of her friends and acquaintances — single mothers, divorcees, married women with inattentive or irresponsible spouses — regularly expressed contempt for their former mates and current partners. She says her confidence was diminished further by female friends who insisted that the press wouldn't receive enough poems to fill a slim volume.

"Even I thought that if I got a book of 100 pages, I would be lucky," she says. "I have this acquaintance, and she said, 'You don't really think you'll find anything, do you?'"

Dr. Madgett says her biggest motivation for compiling the anthology was her overwhelming sense that black women are frustrated with their male mates, friends and family members. "I can hardly have a conversation with black women without the subject of black men coming up," she says. "They really attack black men very often. I don't, and I didn't believe all black women feel that way.

"I know black women have concerns about their relationships with black men," Dr. Madgett says. "All of us have had bad experiences, but there are many, many good men out there."

An author of seven volumes of verse, Dr. Madgett announced the plan for *Adam of Ife* in literary journals. She also solicited poets she'd known over the years. "Ife" (pronounced "ee-fay") refers to a city in Nigerian mythology where the creation took place, Dr. Madgett says. She wanted the title to evoke curiosity and show readers how special black men are. Writers liked the idea. In the end, Dr. Madgett published poems penned by 55 writers who lovingly celebrate the lives of ordinary and extraordinary black men. "I couldn't include most of what I received," she says.

'People do a double take when they look at the book. The sales have just taken off.'

■ ■ ■ ■ ■ ■ ■ ■ ■ ■ ■

Reaction from readers has been terrific, too. Dr. Madgett says several bookstores have placed second orders, and dozens of readers have written and phoned the 20-year-old press. "There's been nothing like this," Dr. Madgett says. "People do a double take when they look at the book. The sales have just taken off. Companies that usually order two to three copies of a title are ordering 20."

Lotus, which printed 2,000 copies of *Adam*, plans a second printing of 3,000 copies before summer. The book also has generated suggestions for spinoffs, a first for the all-poetry publisher. "Male readers have called to ask whether Lotus is planning a similar volume by men about black women," Dr. Madgett says. "I won't rule it out."

Adam of Ife has arrived at a time when black Americans are grappling with the implications of sexual harassment accusations against U.S. Supreme Court Justice Clarence Thomas and the rape conviction of former heavyweight boxing champion Mike Tyson. The debates ignited by the cases are partly fueled by painful sexual politics that haven't received needed attention, says Dallas clinical psychologist Brenda Wall.

Dr. Wall, who has produced self-help video and audio tapes on black male-female relationships, says that the reception of *Adam of Ife* demonstrates that African Americans are pausing to examine sexual politics and their impact on the black community.

'I wanted to say to a younger generation of black women that every relationship with a black male doesn't have to be sexual.'

■ ■ ■ ■ ■ ■ ■ ■ ■ ■

"There is a growing determination to look beyond the frustration and to heal the scars caused by painful relationships," she says. "All sisters and brothers can identify with the scars, but there are increasing numbers of people who believe that we can become empowered to resolve our conflicts."

Vivian Verdell Gordon, a social psychologist who contributed two poems to the anthology under her pen name, Satiafa, hopes her entries help readers restore faith in the opposite sex. *Coach* honors Dr. Gordon's father, a trainer of Olympic track star Jesse Owens. Her second poem, *For Haki*, is dedicated to poet Haki Madhubuti, publisher of Third World Press in Chicago.

A professor at the State University of New York at Albany, Dr. Gordon conducts seminars nationwide for black men and women interested in overcoming hostility and communication problems in relationships. She says the poems can serve as a handbook for discussion. "I wanted to say to a younger generation of black women that every relationship with a black male doesn't have to be sexual, and it doesn't have to be hostile," Dr. Gordon says. "I want them to realize that there are African-American men who are solid people."

Maryland poet Toi Derricotte, who contributed three poems to the anthology, also believes the book will stimulate dialogue between black men and women. She sees its theme as an affirmation of beliefs she's developed in recent years. "My writing has been, I would say, very much about digging up the pain that takes place in the black family," Ms. Derricotte says. "There's a lot of anger toward black men as absent figures and men as violent figures in my work. At this point in my life it's very important for me to talk with black men."

Ms. Derricotte's poems *In Knowledge of Young Boys, Before Making Love* and *The Polishers of Brass* pay homage to her son, her husband and a group of ordinary black men who earn their living polishing the brass fixtures that adorn buildings in the tony Georgetown section of Washington, D.C.

Poets of all ages and experience levels participated in the anthology. Dr. Madgett says two of the youngest still live at home with their parents, and some of the older poets are retired from teaching and other professions. Several, such as critically acclaimed poets Melba Joyce Boyd, Jayne Cortez, Ms. Derricotte, Nikki Giovanni and Louisiana poet laureate Pinkie Gordon Lane, are widely published. Others are just beginning their careers in verse.

Ms. Boyd, director of African-American Studies at the University of Michigan-Flint, admires the mix of poets found in *Adam of Ife*. "Combining well-known writers with beginners is a great way to keep our literature alive," she says.

Author of four volumes of poetry, Ms. Boyd says she also sees the anthology as an opportunity to record an alternative view of black history. "There is a tendency in this country for literature to be critical of black men," Ms. Boyd says. "Some of the criticism is well-founded. A lot of the criticism is lopsided. My poems are about men who have exemplified exceptional integrity or made a sacrifice for black Americans. What the book does is illuminate those men who have defied stereotypes."

April 7, 1992

Well Versed

■ ■ ■ ■ ■ ■ ■ ■ ■ ■

Drawn blinds. Free weights. Dusty carpet. Stuffed chair. Scattered pennies. Notebooks and a black cat named Moon. This is a poet's place. A city space where Tim Seibles works and sometimes spends the night.

Mr. Seibles, who is 36, burrows into his Dallas studio the way most workers settle at their desks: every day, like clockwork. In the past year, his diligence has been rewarded with widening audiences and increasing acclaim. Once considered a local poet, Mr. Seibles is now earning praise and prizes from across the country.

He is looking forward to the publication of his second collection, *Hurdy-Gurdy*, by the Poetry Center of Cleveland State University. Soon he will pack up his studio and move temporarily to Province-town, Mass., for a coveted residency at the Fine Arts Work Center — an artists' colony that has provided refuge for Eugene O'Neill and Edna St. Vincent Millay. A year ago, he received a prestigious National Endowment for the Arts Creative Writing Fellowship — one of 97 granted from a pool of 2,300 applicants. The fellowship is the same that funded the efforts of Alice Walker, Isaac Bashevis Singer, John Gardner, Raymond Carver and dozens of literary lu-minaries early in their careers. "Oh, it's a sweetie," Mr. Seibles says.

As a college freshman in Dallas 18 years ago, Timothy Seibles didn't stride onto the Southern Methodist University campus ready to write. He was prepared to have fun, dazzle football fans and wor-ship legendary coach Hayden Fry.

"I never really thought he'd turn out to be a writer," says his mother, Barbara Seibles. "All he talked about was football."

Coach Fry, revered for prepping players for the pros, was fired the year before the tight end got to campus. A season of frustration followed. "I never got the ball," Mr. Seibles remembers. "It was miserable. I'd wanted to play football and write novels in the off-seasons. My father wanted me to major in poli sci and go to law school. I did, for about a semester."

For him, the most happening place on campus was his creative-writing class, taught by Jack Myers, a young poet who would read poems before the day's lesson. "Jack would read something, and it would hit me," Mr. Seibles recalls. "I wanted to be able to write something with that kind of force."

For nearly two decades, Mr. Seibles has experimented with sonnets, ballads, villanelles and other forms. He favors the challenge of free verse. "For the most part, I don't like formal poems," Mr. Seibles says. "Even in free verse, there is form. There's just a subtler, more dynamic sense of form, that's all.

"As a poem evolves as an idea, as the content begins to take shape, if you're listening carefully and if you're paying attention, it will ask for a certain form on the page. You will think certain things: Short lines. Long lines. Rhyming. Not rhyming. You will sense it. You can sense, this should be in couplets. This should have eight-line stanzas. It's like you're discovering the poem, and that to me is more exciting than working on a form that's already sitting there."

While Mr. Seibles' lines contain some recognizable meters, his poetry defies neat description. An instinctive poet with a propensity for romantic, humanistic and humorous themes, he writes about rain, the earth, the moon, nature, friendship, male-female relationships, football, basketball, Martina Navratilova, childhood, race, sex and everything in between. If there is a thread in his body of work, it is a certain softness in his observations, it is the unmistakable voice of narrators who care whether you listen, and it is the accessible language and ideas.

He writes about rain, friendship, race, football, basketball, sex and everything in between.

■ ■ ■ ■ ■ ■ ■ ■ ■ ■

"When he was at SMU, he never wrote about the black experience," Mr. Myers says. "He would avoid that. I said, 'It must be strange for you to go through SMU. There are so few blacks here.'" But Mr. Seibles has never allowed racial themes to take over his work. "I think we should battle against all forms of evil," he says, "be it the system that is willing to wage war — the way ours seems to be — or a mainstream that wants to exclude people who are dark."

On the other hand, Mr. Seibles asks, "How could you be black and never say anything about race?"

In *Shape*, Mr. Seibles' narrator angrily confronts apartheid:
... I have
a blow-gun
made from the hollow body
of a Bic and one dart tipped
with the piss
of an angel
so angry that even God
sits down when she dances ...

"I think to be consumed with race almost binds you to your oppression ...," Mr. Seibles adds. "To me, it's like saying, 'Yes, I have allowed white people to define my agenda for me. I have allowed white people and white culture to say: You will not talk about (other) things because we have oppressed you successfully, and this is your topic to deal with from now on'... I'll be damned if I'm not going to write about the stars because I'm black ... The stars are here for me, too."

■

As a student at SMU, Mr. Seibles would sign "The Phantom" on notes to his writing teacher, Mr. Myers. "He was a very romantic student," Mr. Myers says. "He was highly romantic. Still is. Everything he writes is straight from the heart."

Mr. Seibles' romance with words began long before he discovered girls, years before he came to Dallas, says his mother. Mrs. Seibles, a Philadelphia high school English teacher, tested her teaching theories on her younger son and his brother, Thomas Jr. She didn't just read to her children, she required them to read to her.

"Probably more influential than any religious figure would be the writing my mom would read to me as a child," Mr. Seibles says. "My first attraction to the cadence of language at all was through her."

By the time he entered second grade, Tim was writing science-fiction stories and insisting that his mother type them. His father, Thomas Seibles Sr., a government research biochemist, also jumped into the act. The boys produced a daily newspaper, for which their dad paid them 10 cents each. The family's home-based publishing hobby taught Tim his most valuable lesson: "I never thought only white people could write great things," he says.

Mrs. Seibles remembers her younger son as an insatiable reader. "It was very difficult to have a book to yourself," Mrs. Seibles says. "He'd always pick it up and read behind me. He would always ask if it was good. I'd tell him no. But he caught on to that."

Reading still fills the gaps between writing, family, pick-up basketball games and tennis. African-American literature is alphabetically arranged on the top shelves of a studio bookcase. There are two shelves of poetry by Octavio Paz, Pablo Neruda, Rita Dove, W.S. Merwin and others; three shelves of fiction, including stories and novels by Alice Walker, Charles Johnson and Jeanette Winterson. Fantasy and science fiction fill two more shelves. The works of James Baldwin, Gandhi, Ralph Waldo Emerson, Salman Rushdie, Ernest Becker, Bell Hooks and Harry and Bonaro Overstreet fill the bottom rows.

Mr. Seibles does more than read, though. He studies words. When asked how he developed the rhythm of one of his most hilarious poems, *The Ballad of Sadie LaBabe*, he effortlessly recites passages from *Molly Means*, a ballad by Margaret Walker Alexander:

Molly Means was a hag and a witch
Chile of the devil, the dark and sitch ...
Imp at three and wench at 'leben
She counted her husbands to the number seben ...

At a party for Mr. Merwin, Mr. Seibles enchanted the poet and awed other guests by reciting the 1971 Pulitzer Prize winner's poetry. "Merwin just loved it," Mr. Myers says. "It was the highest form of flattery."

Reading and reciting have enhanced Mr. Seibles' work immea-
surably, Mr. Myers says. "He pens accomplished, highly narrative
poems," Mr. Myers says. "In the beginning, he was a lyric poet. Now
he's kind of a lyric storyteller. He's not just writing songs. He's making statements with depth and breadth."

◼

On an unusually pleasant summer evening, the South Dallas Cultural Center auditorium is half full. The evening is quadruple-billed:
Tim Seibles; his wife, dancer Fern Tresvan; dancer David Wilson,
and guitarist Carlo Pezzimenti.

Mr. Seibles' poetry takes on a liveliness not apparent in print. His
reading timbre is a personal style more inviting than mere ono-
matopoeia, beyond Elizabethan affectations. He moseys through
Big Mouth and Looking, imbuing their sounds with a quiet lilt, a low
moan, a high near-holler or a soft chuckle. The wave of words
evokes laughter or chills, even tears — always applause. The audience of about a hundred nods and claps with the requisite reverence
during the dance and guitar performances. But, at the end, it is Mr.
Seibles who is surrounded by smitten listeners. As he sits on a bench,
the fans congratulate him, they inquire about promises of publication, they ask him to autograph their copies of his book. Ms. Tresvan, about 15 feet away, speaks up: "Tim, did you tell Phyllis the
good news?"

"What good news?" Mr. Seibles asks.

"About *Hurdy-Gurdy?*"

"Oh yeah," says Mr. Seibles, smiling his trademark big smile.

He turns to tell the woman next to him, one of his many devoted
fans, about his publishing victory. Like a rock groupie, the woman
jumps into the air and begins to shriek. "Yes, yes!"

◼

Mr. Seibles' dark, musty studio, littered with broken-down furni-
ture, pawn tickets, fliers and old books, is stocked with enough juice,
rice cakes and paper for a few days' survival. A stack of record al-

bums — Jimi Hendrix, Run DMC, Bach, Wynton Marsalis, Bobby McFerrin, Parliament, Funkadelic, Public Enemy, Andres Segovia and Brian Eno — leans against one wall.

None of the possessions reveal anything about Mr. Seibles the husband and father, brother and son. He married Ms. Tresvan, who teaches dance at a Dallas high school, seven years ago; the couple met 10 years ago when she stopped him on the street to ask him where she might find an apartment in University Park. The couple have a 10-month-old son, Kade, named after a lusty character who appears in two of Mr. Seibles' ballads.

Ms. Tresvan says she's untroubled by her husband's time in the studio. "All writers require a great deal of privacy, a lot of solitude," Ms. Tresvan says. "Having always worked with artists, I don't have a problem with that."

Husband and wife often give collaborative performances; his first book, *Body Moves*, seems influenced by dance, femininity and sensuality. "I'm fascinated by our relationship to our bodies," Mr. Seibles says.

Lean, tall and broad-shouldered, Mr. Seibles is built like the professional athlete he once hoped to become. He usually wears sneakers, baggy shirts and baggier pants — uncomplicated clothes that allow him to hop on the 10-speed propped against the studio wall whenever he needs some exercise, whenever a change of scenery might help him shake loose a buried idea. The wardrobe also represents the spartan life he

He pays his bills with poems, and they don't earn much.

■ ■ ■ ■ ■ ■ ■ ■ ■ ■

lives. The Chevy Nova, which he's owned since 1977, completes the picture.

He pays his bills with poems, and they don't earn much. "I live very cheaply," he says. "I have to."

Hurdy-Gurdy will earn the author "50 free copies, a lump royalty of $300 and 50 percent discount on any additional copies of the book" he wants to buy, according to the contest notification letter. *Body Moves*, Mr. Seibles' first collection, now in its second printing, has sold 1,500 copies — a lot, say those in the profession, for a relatively unknown poet.

Mr. Seibles last held a regular, full-time job 15 months ago, when he taught English at the Episcopal School of Dallas. Before that, he spent several years teaching high school English in the Dallas Independent School District. Since devoting himself to full-time writing, Mr. Seibles has been buoyed by grants, reading honorariums, the rare publication royalty, contest winnings and earnings from occasional essays. Like generations before him, Mr. Seibles peddles his own poetry. He bound his most popular poem, *The Ballad of Sadie LaBabe*, into a typewritten chapbook with illustrations by his buddy James Sharper. "I've probably sold I don't know how many copies," Mr. Seibles says. "In stores, they sell them for $4, plus tax. When I'm selling them on my own, I just sell them for $3 straight. I don't have to deal with anyone else's percentage."

To date, criticism has amounted to verbal raves and standing-room-only audiences of local fans. Despite its success and the writer's rising reputation, there are no reviews of his work. Putting this into perspective, Tim Seibles is modest, even self-deprecating. "I'm not important enough."

March 15, 1992

Out of the Ashes

■ ■ ■ ■ ■ ■ ■ ■ ■ ■

L OS ANGELES — As Jean Collins watched the Aquarian Bookshop burn to the ground, she was consumed with feelings of anger and of loss.

"You should have seen the looks of cruelty on their faces," she said, recalling the rioters who torched the bookstore where she worked for nine years. "You should have been there to see them as they drove their cars into the iron gates and destroyed the life work of other people. No amount of money can ever replace what was here."

News of the Aquarian Bookshop's destruction — the result of rioting after four white Los Angeles police officers were found not guilty in the beating of black motorist Rodney King — stunned this city's literary community. It galvanized a national network of admirers connected only by their love of literature and devotion to the Aquarian, the country's oldest continuously operated black-owned bookstore.

Richard Bray, director of an international writers' group called PEN Center U.S.A. West, said that although all independent bookstores are "endangered species," the loss of Aquarian is particularly devastating.

"There are so few African-American bookstores in this country," Mr. Bray said. "The idea that the oldest — the very symbol of ideas and education — was destroyed is like someone killed all of our hope."

'You should have been there to see them as they drove their cars into the iron gates and destroyed the life work of other people.'

■ ■ ■ ■ ■ ■ ■ ■ ■ ■

Lost in the fire were more than $200,000 in uninsured books and other assets, including a rare print from Texas artist John Biggers and a collection of Tarot books. The blaze also wiped out a center of solace for thousands of Los Angeles residents and a West Coast home for dozens of celebrated writers, including Maya Angelou, Margaret Walker Alexander, Rosa Guy and Haki Madhubuti.

A week after the two days of rioting, friends of the Aquarian had called from as far away as New York to express their condolences. Many dropped by in person to pledge their help in rebuilding the institution owned by Alfred and Bernice Ligon, the enigmatic couple who changed many of their lives.

Dr. Richard King, a Durham, N.C., psychiatrist, recalled the store and spiritual center as a haven for cultural exchange, progressive politics and metaphysical instruction. He met Dr. Ligon, 86, and Mrs. Ligon, 79, when he was an undergraduate student during the 1960s.

'It was a psychic experience. I felt that some part of me was being fed there.'

■ ■ ■ ■ ■ ■ ■ ■ ■ ■

"When I was a resident in San Francisco, I would fly to L.A. for class there every Saturday, then fly back that night," Dr. King said. "This will sound philosophical, but it was a psychic experience. I felt that some part of me was being fed there."

Most people who visited the Aquarian quickly found that it offered more than books. During the 1960s, the Ligons displayed their books on portable shelves, which could be moved to provide room for a 50-seat theater. They welcomed socialists, communists and mainstream political groups who met there to discuss current events.

At night and on weekends, classes on esoteric psychology, astrology and mysticism filled the center with reverent students. The classes, which cost $2 per session, proved so popular that the couple moved the bookstore to a larger location several blocks away, in the Martin Luther King Boulevard shopping center, where it burned in the riots.

Earl Ofari Hutchinson, author of *Black Fatherhood: The Guide to*

Male Parenting, is one of many Los Angeles-area artists who formed an ad hoc committee to comfort the Ligons and rebuild the bookstore.

"We all must remember that Aquarian has been a force in this community," Mr. Hutchinson told Dr. Ligon a week after the riots. "I feel like I owe you something for all the years you've contributed to our collective well-being."

The sentiments were repeated throughout the day. By early afternoon, Ms. Collins, the bookstore's secretary and administrative assistant, had filled several pages of a yellow legal pad with the names of people who called to offer help.

Dr. Ligon founded the Aquarian in 1941 with his sister Jeni, a former MGM dancer. They opened shop with $50 in used books in a south-central Los Angeles storefront, beneath an apartment the two of them shared. When it burned, it contained 10,000 different titles that spanned a wide range of African-American and spiritual topics. From the beginning, Dr. Ligon recalled, the Aquarian's mission was to enrich African Americans. For those who couldn't buy books, the Ligons rented copies for a few pennies each day.

Dr. Ligon, a man of carefully chosen words, was philosophical about a loss many consider monumental. "It's part of a cycle," he said quietly. "This rebellion was bound to happen, and I imagine many young people feel very proud that they stood up."

A slender, cinnamon-skinned man who has taught metaphysical philosophy for decades, he said that he had planned to sell the store in the months ahead to pursue several writing and archival projects. After five decades, he said, he and his wife were ready to move on.

"Our lease was up this upcoming month," Dr. Ligon said. "Things were very slow over the last 18 months. There's this recession, you know. And when you have bookshops in the black community, how many people are going to buy books when they worry about buying groceries?"

But area writers and artists are reluctant to accept the notion of a Los Angeles without an Aquarian Bookshop. A few days after the fire, a group met with the Ligons to coordinate fund-raising efforts aimed at reopening the Aquarian as a non-profit enterprise. Members of the group said they would contact black celebrities about participating in a series of fund-raisers for the bookstore. Mr. Hutchinson promised to buy newspaper advertisements announcing the store's demise and its planned rebirth. "The more information people have," he said, "the more funds we can generate."

The group's commitment typified the devotion expressed by many who called and visited after the fire. The Ligons' openness enabled them to form close bonds with people across the city's race, cultural and class lines, said Maybie Settlage, a white science teacher at nearby Carver Junior High School.

"People saw they (the rioters) hit the chicken place and said, 'Too bad,'" Ms. Suttlage said. "The car repair shop was burned and people said, 'Oh, well.' People cried about this. Real, watery tears."

'People cried about this. Real, watery tears.'

■ ■ ■ ■ ■ ■ ■ ■ ■ ■

Among the Ligons' supporters are book publishers, who praise the couple's business acumen. "They've had the same employees for years, and bookstores are not known for competitive salaries," said Peggy Keller, marketing manager for Random House. "Independent bookstores are the backbone of this industry. And Al and Bernice always listened openly to our suggestions. They were always willing to let our writers speak there. And they were an absolute dream when it came to paying their bills."

Random House, longtime publisher of African-American writers such as Toni Morrison and John Edgar Wideman, has agreed to donate free books to the Aquarian and has pledged to extend credit for up to a year after the store reopens. Other offers of support have come from the American Booksellers Association and the Southern California Booksellers Association.

"Al and Bernice are two of the warmest people I've ever known," Ms. Keller said. "If we all had their attitude, maybe none of this (rioting) would have ever happened."

May 7, 1992

Black, White
and Read All Over

■ ■ ■ ■ ■ ■ ■ ■ ■ ■

I f there are literary epiphanies, Charlene Wilson Howell had hers while reading James Baldwin's *Go Tell It On The Mountain*.

"It was just a religious experience for me," she says.

It dawned on her then, in 1969, that there was an entire canon of literature, a whole culture omitted from serious scholarship and the fabric of American life.

"Growing up in South Carolina, you get the feeling you know black culture," Mrs. Howell says. "Reading the literature, I found I didn't know the culture at all."

The discovery started Mrs. Howell, an Anglo homemaker, on an intensive exploration of African-American literature that has lasted more than two decades. Her relationship with the genre reached a zenith of sorts this year, when a Dallas community college hosted a contemporary African-American literary conference that she spent a year organizing.

Mr. Baldwin's autobiographical novel somehow reconnected Mrs. Howell, who is 46, to images she remembered from her childhood in Charleston. The city always had a large African-American population, but was segregated throughout her childhood. Blacks she encountered often were the colorfully clad women who peddled flowers from corner carts in the picturesque seaside city. Radio was her only regular exposure.

"I listened to the Morgan Street AME Church services on the radio," Mrs. Howell says. "I loved it."

Although she discovered Mr. Baldwin's book during the turbulent '60s, the country's political climate had failed to affect her reading selections. Or ignite her activism. An intense student, she attended classes at the College of Charleston in a vacuum, virtually untouched by events in the world around her.

"My education was extremely narrow," she says, a hint of dismay creeping into her voice. "It exposed me to three basic kinds of literature: English, American and French."

Still, she recalls the small liberal arts college as a wonderful choice. The interdisciplinary programs allowed her to indulge her love for history, languages and literature.

Mrs. Howell is a methodical reader. Like others, she keeps lists of books she wants to read. Unlike others, she reads them. Slashes are drawn through fading titles in a tiny, six-ring green notebook she keeps at her side. Almost every day, she adds to the list. She also pens reports about each work. The reports, on big index cards stored in a shoebox-size file, summarize the plot. They also analyze the characters, examine the narrative structure, discuss the theme and reflect on whether the work is successful.

Like others, she keeps lists of books she wants to read. Unlike others, she reads them.

■ ■ ■ ■ ■ ■ ■ ■ ■ ■

"The thought that she might not remember compels her to keep reports like she does," says close friend Barbara Weinstein. "The reports are a kind of tangible thing that is left."

Mrs. Howell prefers keeping reports to keeping books. Unlike most bibliophiles who amass weighty collections, she donates her books to the Dallas Public Library, where she serves as vice chairwoman of the advisory board.

"A lot of my books are unusual — ones they don't have," she says. "Good books are to be shared with friends and fellow readers."

Mrs. Howell can't remember what ignited her lifelong love for the written word. Her parents, a career Navy officer and a homemaker, were not voracious readers.

"The bookmobile came two times a week," she remembers. "We were allowed to take 10 books. One summer I read five volumes of World Book."

She taught herself to read before she turned 6. Her mother

gasped one day when she found young Charlene reading a grim newspaper account of the execution of Ethel and Julius Rosenberg. If Mrs. Howell's thirst for prose sometimes startled her parents, the passion provided ample early rewards. As a 12-year-old, her parents granted written permission for her to check out books from the public library's adult section. "I had to make a plea on bended knee," she says.

Librarians, however, retained the right to censor the authors loaned to impressionable young minds. Romantic mysteries by Daphne du Maurier were among the approved works. Little Charlene devoured Ms. du Maurier's works. When she was 14, she found the writer's home address in a 10-year-old copy of *Ladies Home Journal*. She wrote the writer in England. Better yet, the writer wrote back.

Mrs. Howell spends part of each day reading. The pastime usually is taken up in bed. When her husband wants to sleep, she clicks off the headboard lamp and attaches one of those tiny clamp-on lights to her book. During the day, she snuggles on her sofa, reading with the aid of the sunlight that bathes her large living room. "Most of us don't read," says Ms. Weinstein. "She reads all the time."

Mrs. Howell reads African literature from all over the continent and is nearly as passionate about Japanese literature as she is about African-American literature. One of her favorite authors is 19th-century English novelist Anthony Trollope. Friends who wanted a list of books by Naguib Mahfouz knew who to call when the Egyptian author won the 1988 Nobel Prize for literature. "Why she had read him, I don't know," says Ms. Weinstein. "She's a wonderful information system. When someone needs to know something, holy cow, we say, 'Let's ask Charlene.'"

But that hardly means Mrs. Howell is a pampered homemaker who sits around and reads all day. She devotes the same thoroughness to a number of pursuits. With Warren, her husband of 23 years, Mrs. Howell refurbished the antique grand piano that sits elegantly in the corner of her spacious living room. "Playing," she says, "is the most pleasant way to pass time next to reading."

She counts visual arts, theater and politics among her other interests and manages to reserve time for the League of Women Voters and various local civic committees. "Her opinion is respected in professional circles," says Max Wells, the Dallas City Council member who reappointed Mrs. Howell to the library board.

In fact, friends describe Mrs. Howell as a woman of action. Once she gets an idea or makes a decision, doubters need not attempt to distract her. "She's persistent," says Patrick O'Brien, director of the Dallas Public Library. "When she says she's going to do something, she does it. Having been in the business for 25 years, I've run into all kinds of voracious readers. Few follow through the way Charlene does."

Take literary lioness Toni Morrison. The Pulitzer Prize-winning fiction writer is very selective about where she speaks. She'd turned down speaking invitations from Southern Methodist University and was unavailable to appear at the Dallas Museum of Art during the "Black Art: Ancestral Legacy" exhibit. Somehow, some way, Charlene Howell got Toni Morrison to be a featured participant in the conference she had organized.

Her vast knowledge has not created a haughty intellectual.

■ ■ ■ ■ ■ ■ ■ ■ ■ ■

"Toni Morrison is a real feather in Charlene Howell's cap," Mr. O'Brien says.

The conference was born out of concern as much as Mrs. Howell's love for literature. It nagged her that literature never emerged as a diplomatic tool when Dallas Together, a citywide task force, suggested solutions for racial disharmony.

"Factual books will give the facts of a people or the facts of a country," she says. "But if you want to know their souls, you have to read the literature."

Eventually, it occurred to her to turn her vision into a reality. Mrs. Howell and a committee organized the daylong conference, which attracted registrants from as far away as the West Texas city of Midland.

Her vast knowledge has not created a haughty intellectual. In fact, she's anything but a bookwormish bore. After plying guests with just-baked peanut-butter cookies, she slips off her pumps and curls her stocking feet beneath her. It cracks her up that she spent a week searching for a sumptuous crab-stuffed shrimp recipe requested by Ms. Morrison. She found the recipe, then faxed it to Fairmont Hotel chef Avner Samuel. With the success of the conference behind her, she looks forward to her next literary project.

"You know," she whispers, "I'd love to have a Japanese literature conference. But don't tell my husband."

April 4, 1990

SECTION V

■

AGAINST ALL ODDS

●●●●●●●●●●

The Sins
of the Son

■■■■■■■■■

Whenever an ambulance sped by Betty Johnson's Dallas apartment at night, her body would stiffen and she would sit up in the darkness. Each night, a fitful sleep washed over her as she waited for her youngest son to come home.

Sometimes Kevin, then 14, wouldn't return for days. And when he did, he promised never to worry his mother again.

Kevin's absences became so frequent, Mrs. Johnson says, that she called county juvenile authorities and asked to have her son picked up and put in detention. "They told me they couldn't come get him," Mrs. Johnson says. "They said he hadn't done anything wrong."

It wasn't long before he did.

Kevin Johnson, now 19, was arrested for drug and weapon possession outside a Dallas crack house in 1988. What he remembers most about the arrest is the phone call police made to his mother as they drove him to Dallas County's juvenile detention center.

'I probably kind of made her feel like she was a bad mother.'

■■■■■■■■■

"I could hear her crying," Kevin recalls. "She seemed kind of relieved that she knew where I was. I probably kind of made her feel like she was a bad mother."

Both Kevin and Mrs. Johnson acknowledge that their relationship and their lives might have been different if she had had more control over her children.

Some community leaders and public officials blame much of the violence committed by juveniles on what they believe is an abdication of parental responsibility. But parents like Mrs. Johnson say those leaders, officials and other critics fail to recognize the challenge of raising children in a violent society, one that offers few social services and little crisis intervention for families.

Violent youths make headlines. And it's easy to point the finger of blame at the family, at the heads of the household. It's a convenient conclusion, until you look behind the headlines and the police statistics; until you come face to face with the desperate parents who are trying to cope with children who have become entangled in a web of criminal behavior.

Until you hear Betty Jean Johnson's story.

■ A working mother

At first glance, it's hard to tell that Betty Johnson raised six children alone after being widowed nearly 20 years ago. At 53, she is as wrinkle-free and slender as a childless woman half her age. But though her face is gentle and kind, her hands hint at a lifetime of hard labor. The skin folds and ripples around bony knuckles and prominent veins.

Except for the four years when she received welfare benefits, Mrs. Johnson has been a working mother. She says she turned to public assistance after she had difficulty making ends meet with her earnings from "day work," the only employment she could find with an eighth-grade education.

"I made maybe $25 a day cleaning houses, but you was never guaranteed work," she explains. "Money was always a problem."

The food stamps and monthly government allowance weren't enough, either.

Finally, 15 years ago, Mrs. Johnson found a permanent, full-time job with benefits working in the laundry room at Presbyterian Hospital. The job solved many of her financial woes, but it created another set of problems.

"I had to get up at 4:10 every morning to catch the 5:23 bus," Mrs. Johnson says. Her children were responsible for getting themselves to school in the mornings. It was usually dark by the time she returned.

"My sister or one of my brothers was usually home when I got there," Kevin says. "My mother always told me to do my homework before I turned on the TV or went outside."

By the time Mrs. Johnson started working at Presbyterian, her oldest son, Anthony, already had legal troubles. Energy not spent working and caring for her younger children was used to keep a distance between Anthony and the rest of the family.

Anthony, Mrs. Johnson says, became a "bad child" after her husband died in a car accident almost two decades ago. "He was rough," she says of Anthony, who died at age 27. "He did everything. He was into drugs — sniffing paint and shooting heroin.

"Ten years ago, a guy shot him in the back of the head. It blew his brains out. He died. He was just a bad child, just rotten to the core."

Mrs. Johnson isn't sure whether her younger sons looked up to Anthony. She isn't sure how his behavior influenced them.

Vincent, 28, a forklift operator for a bottled water company, has never been in trouble, Mrs. Johnson says.

Rickey, 31, is serving a 60-year sentence for burglary in a state prison in Tennessee Colony. Steven, 30, is serving a life sentence for burglary and aggravated robbery in Huntsville.

Rickey's twin, Vicky, lives on her own, her mother says.

"I always told myself when I got grown, I would make sure my kids ate and dressed better than I did," Mrs. Johnson says.

"I always told the kids I didn't want them to come up like me and be forced to slave

> **'I always told myself when I got grown, I would make sure my kids ate and dressed better than I did.'**
>
> ■■■■■■■■■■

hard in a laundry. I wanted them to get a good education and find good jobs."

Mrs. Johnson wanted better for her children because she didn't have much growing up in South Dallas. Her mother worked in a restaurant. She doesn't discuss her father.

As a teen-ager, she married a young construction worker, a "boy from the neighborhood," and started having children. The early marriage and fast-growing family limited her opportunities.

"I was just a girl," she says. "I didn't know what I was doing from the first to the last."

Mrs. Johnson did know that hard work — honest, even low-paying work — paved the way to a respectable life. But her sons' tastes, which she believes may have been influenced by friends and television, were much more expensive than she could afford.

After 15 years on the job, she makes slightly more than $6 an hour. What she couldn't buy, the boys either took or stole money or sold drugs to get.

"I always told them, 'What the Lord don't give me with a job, I don't need to have,'" she says. "I always said, 'Why can't you be like me? I ain't never been in any trouble.'"

It's not a question Kevin finds easy to answer.

■ A career of crime

At 5-foot-9 and with a muscular build, Kevin takes pride in his appearance. His jeans are beltless and stylishly baggy. The pants have sharp military creases, ironed in, at his instruction, by the local dry cleaners. He wears a gold hoop in his left ear and a Notre Dame University T-shirt.

He is polite and matter-of-fact as he recounts his life of crime. He repeats that criminal activities are part of his past.

"That's behind me," Kevin says. "I really don't like to talk about it."

When Kevin isn't sleeping, he thumbs through trade-school catalogs, looks for jobs and visits his current girlfriend and their 1-year-old daughter. He plans to move in with her after he finds a job.

Kevin, who dropped out of high school in the 10th grade, has a baby boy by another young woman he no longer sees. He provides what he can — disposable diapers, milk, clothes — for both children.

"Every time I apply for a job, they want a high school diploma," he says.

He's had five jobs since being released from the Texas Youth Commission in 1989. Most of the jobs have been in warehouses and have required a lot of lifting. The best-paying job earned him $5 per hour, with no benefits.

Although the money hardly compares with his haul as a drug dealer, he has refused to be tempted by friends who are still in the business.

"At first when I got out, I seen them," Kevin says. "They be saying, 'Yeah, man, you gonna be back. You want to make money, don't you? You wanna get back into it?' I said, 'No.'"

Mrs. Johnson says she's heard "no" before. She is worried that Kevin won't be able to resist the temptations unless he finds steady work or enrolls in school.

"These young people not working, they're bound to get in trouble," she says.

Kevin says his mother has always worried — mostly about things she could do nothing about. What she's been unable to do, he says, is understand.

She never understood peer pressure, he says. In Kevin's view, she never understood the status that goes with flashy clothes and pocketfuls of money; never understood the need for the respect and power that goes with wealth.

"I was making more money than my mother," Kevin says. "It kind of made me feel like I was somebody. I kind of wanted to be known. People look up to you. Girls be liking you."

At the height of his career on the streets, Kevin says he was turning a $900-a-day profit pushing crack and cocaine. He spent money on clothes (silk shirts and tailored pants), shoes (expensive leather and $100 sneakers), jewelry (gold chains) and entertainment (movies, video games).

The streets, Kevin says, were exciting. The police were part of the action. "Running from the police was fun," he says. "It was like a game."

■ Doing the best she could

Kevin's brothers wrote him letters from prison warning him to stay out of trouble. He says his brother Vincent and his sister Vicky told him, "You're wrongin' Mama."

Mrs. Johnson lectured, prayed and waited for prison or death to take Kevin. When the boys were young, she punished them. But by the time they reached their teens, they were too big to whip. If she grounded them, they stayed in the house only while she was there.

"I couldn't be with them all the time," she says. "I had to work. I did the best I could on my own. If I could have watched over them more, maybe they would have been much better children."

At one point, she says, she was a wreck. A doctor prescribed Valium, but the drug couldn't calm her, couldn't help her cope with the boys.

"I went through a lot," Mrs. Johnson says. "I almost had a nervous breakdown. I stayed real depressed. The police were just running in and out of my house."

After Steven and Rickey were sent to prison, she focused her attention on Kevin. "I tried to be strict. I talked to him the best I knew how," Mrs. Johnson says.

> '**Despite the fact Kevin got in trouble, you can tell she tried to raise him.**'
>
> ■ ■ ■ ■ ■ ■ ■ ■ ■ ■

When Kevin was sent to Dallas House, a residential rehabilitation center, Mrs. Johnson attended family counseling sessions offered by the Texas Youth Commission.

Robert Louis, a treatment coordinator at the state agency, works with many teens in trouble and their families. He remembers the Johnsons and says he was impressed by Kevin's and Mrs. Johnson's honesty. They spoke openly, Mr. Louis says, and didn't blame the police or juvenile authorities for their problems.

"Despite the fact Kevin got in trouble, you can tell she tried to raise him," Mr. Louis says. "She's a great woman, and she's worked so hard."

It was at the Texas Youth Commission that Mrs. Johnson faced the facts about her parenting skills. "I should have been tougher," she says. "I should have said, 'If you decide you want to get in more trouble, you have to get out of my house.' "

"I should have told them, 'Either you go to school or you get out.' I should have made them look for jobs. I didn't put my foot down enough like I should have."

At the Texas Youth Commission, Kevin realized the depth of his mother's devotion and he decided to live by the law. "It took me getting locked up to learn how much me and my brother put her through. She's done so much for me. She didn't buy things for herself, even stuff she needed, so she could get me what I want.

"I learned that I couldn't have everything I want," Kevin says. "I learned that I couldn't do what I want when I want. I learned the rules. I learned if I don't follow the rules, I go to jail. I didn't like not having my freedom."

Mrs. Johnson has relinquished the guilt she once felt.

A strong male presence is the one thing Mrs. Johnson believes would have made a difference in the lives of her children.

"It would have been easier if I had a good husband," she says. "I was a mother and father to my kids. Maybe that wasn't enough. Maybe I didn't put my foot down enough. I don't know ...."

"I wasn't an unfit mother," she continues. "I didn't drink or take drugs. The kids did the things they did because they wanted to."

February 28, 1993

Robbed

■ ■ ■ ■ ■ ■ ■ ■ ■ ■

J oyce Ann Brown served nine years in prison, and her family and friends shared every second of that sentence.

Her child lost the mother she leaned on. Her mother lost her firstborn daughter. Her siblings lost their big sister. And her friends lost a pool partner, enchilada maker and faithful comrade.

Today Mrs. Brown lives in an abyss of uncertainty, unsure if she should seek work, unsure if she should smile so brightly. Family and friends share her apprehension as she waits for the county to decide whether her 10-year-old armed robbery case should be retried.

Joyce Ann Brown was sentenced to life in prison for a robbery in which two women held up a North Dallas fur store and left the store's owner dead.

The Texas Court of Criminal Appeals last fall set aside Mrs. Brown's conviction because of prosecutorial misconduct, including withholding the fact that the state's chief witness, a jailhouse informant, was a convicted perjurer.

Those who know Joyce Ann Brown best say they also know the most important fact about the case. They know she didn't do it. They know how much their sister has suffered. And they know that their lives will never again be the same.

■ The mother

Two refrigerators line the wall in Ruby Kelley's kitchen, standing as monuments to her contribution to Joyce Ann Brown's nine-year fight for freedom. Those big, square boxes stored many of the supplies that Mrs. Kelley turned into meals that turned into money needed to pay her daughter's legal fees.

When a Dallas defense lawyer promised he could free Mrs. Brown, Mrs. Kelley "scraped and borrowed from kinfolks" to pay the bill.

When that wasn't enough, she paid the $7,500 fee a plate at a time. Week after week, Mrs. Kelley stood before her stove, stewing chitterlings, smothering chicken, sauteing potatoes, frying fish and baking pastries. She prepared hundreds of hot meals and hawked them for $1.50 each on the sidewalks of the Roseland Homes, an East Dallas housing project.

"I never in my life counted on cooking that much food," she says. "We would sell $200 to $300 each weekend."

But Mrs. Kelley also never counted on the phone call that came one afternoon in May 1980. A friend was on the line asking her about an arrest warrant for her oldest daughter.

"She said, 'Honey, have you read the newspaper? Tell me it's not true.'" Mrs. Kelley hastily unfolded her papers and told her friend, "Oh, no. It's not true."

In the months just before the phone call, Mrs. Kelley, 65, had finally begun to relax a little. All but three of her children were grown and gone. Debilitating arthritis had forced her to rest more and cut back on physical activity.

'Honey, have you read the newspaper? Tell me it's not true.'

■ ■ ■ ■ ■ ■ ■ ■ ■ ■

This doctor-ordered respite was well-earned. She had earned it helping her husband raise 10 children with the pittance she received for picking cotton near McKinney. She had earned it by carefully budgeting the wages Robert Kelley earned as a laborer and the money she made working occasionally as a hotel housekeeper.

Mrs. Kelley says her example produced humble, hard-working children. The family is a religious group that has filled the choir stands at Bethlehem Christian Church in McKinney every Sunday since 1952.

"All my boys and all my girls are in the choir," Mrs. Kelley says. "They can sing the hair off your head."

Until Joyce's ordeal, none of her children had been in any trouble, except that, unknown to Mrs. Kelley, Mrs. Brown had been arrested for prostitution.

"I put on a lot of age after Joyce went down," Mrs. Kelley says. "I spent nine Mother's Days away from the other kids to be with her."

Despite her sacrifice, Mrs. Kelley harbors feelings of inadequacy about the way she raised Joyce's daughter, Koquice Spencer, who was 11 when her mother went to prison. Mrs. Kelley later helped Ms. Spencer care for her daughter Brittany, born six years after Mrs. Kelley became a surrogate mother to her granddaughter.

"I did the best I could," says Mrs. Kelley, "but if Joyce had been here, Quice would have been in college and everything."

Only reluctantly will Mrs. Kelley admit that other scars — her pronounced limp and gnarled hands — are wounds from the long war fought for her daughter's freedom. The metal plates that replaced a joint in her right knee and bone in her right hand were partially a result of those hours spent in front of the stove cooking meals for money.

'When I get on my knees at night, I say, "Lord, when is it ever going to be over?" '

■ ■ ■ ■ ■ ■ ■ ■ ■ ■

"I was standing when the doctor told me not to," Mrs. Kelley says. "But when you're poor and you're down and you don't have a dime and you don't know how you'll get one, you've got to do something."

Losing the use of her leg was a small price to pay, Mrs. Kelley says. Losing her daughter forever would have cost much more.

Joyce is home now, but still Mrs. Kelley worries. Mostly, she worries that the Dallas County district attorney's office will retry her daughter.

"When I get on my knees at night, I say, 'Lord, when is it ever going to be over?' "

She lifts her thick glasses to wipe away tears that flow when she talks about fearing the unknown.

"I got on her this evening. I said, 'Joyce, you were out a little later than I want you to be out,' " Mrs. Kelley says. "I tell her to be careful. If I go to bed and she's out of this house, I don't go to sleep unless I know she's at my son's or one of my daughters' houses."

■ The daughter

Koquice Spencer, 21, stops filing her fingernails to pull a pile of papers from her school bag.

"Ooh, Mama, want to see my test?" asks Ms. Spencer, a student at Renee's Cosmetology Center.

"Did you score high?" replies Joyce Ann Brown. "Ninety-two. Well, all right."

Across the pink-on-pink bedroom, mother and daughter beam the same broad smile at one another. They share the same high cheek bones and thick, shiny hair. Although Mrs. Brown is heavier, both women are about 5 feet tall and fairly petite.

It's been nine years since mother and child have been able to touch and talk without being separated by a glass or wire partition. Nine years since a murder conviction defined their roles as prisoner and visitor.

But as happy as both are about being together, mother and daughter sense some tension in this renewed relationship. One minute Ms. Spencer feels like her mother's little girl and the next minute she feels like her mother's mother.

"Me and my mother, we're trying to ... get on that right track," Ms. Spencer says. "I was sick and she told me, 'You can't go out.' I said, 'You can't tell me I can't go out. I'm grown, Mama.'"

More unsettling about her mother's homecoming are the reporters who phone day and night begging for interviews. Because her own anonymity is quickly vanishing, Ms. Spencer slips away when journalists come looking for her mother.

"I run off and hide," she says. "I feel like I know all of Dallas and half of Fort Worth when I go out. People walk up to me and say, 'I saw you on TV.' I feel embarrassed."

In the years between Ms. Spencer's 12th and 21st birthdays, her emotions ranged from acceptance to despair. She revealed little of this turmoil in the many letters she mailed to her mother. She disclosed even less during biweekly visits to the Mountain View Unit of

ONE VOICE ■ TONI Y. JOSEPH

the Texas Department of Corrections prison in Gatesville.

Ms. Spencer still doesn't like to talk about those years, and when she finally does, it's a matter-of-fact presentation of an incredibly poignant tale. Mrs. Brown's conviction meant that her daughter had to move from their spacious home in the Dallas suburb of Garland to her grandparents' crowded housing-project apartment. The move meant having to sacrifice many of the suburban childhood privileges she'd come to expect.

"Where I was attending school in Garland, I was a cheerleader," Ms. Spencer says. "I was the only black cheerleader. I was involved in many activities when my mom was here: Girl Scouts, jazz dance, gymnastics, you name it. I moved from where there were mixed races to the projects."

The move meant having to sacrifice many of the privileges she'd come to expect.

■ ■ ■ ■ ■ ■ ■ ■ ■ ■

Although Ms. Spencer's grandparents showered her with affection, they had passed their child-rearing days and had few resources to provide her the kind of lifestyle she was accustomed to.

"I always thought, 'What would my life be like if my mother was here?'"

Ms. Spencer says she probably wouldn't have become a teen mom.

"I knew I was loved by my parents, and I knew my grandparents loved me," she says, "but I wanted someone who loved me no matter what."

So she gave birth to Brittany Spencer nearly four years ago while enrolled at Hillcrest High School. She ran in a track meet two weeks after her daughter was born and went on to graduate with her class. Today she spends her time balancing motherhood, a full-time course of study and a part-time switchboard operator's job at the Hotel Crescent Court.

The separation, she says, "just wasn't right."

Once at school, officials suspended her after she decked a girl who said unkind things about Mrs. Brown.

"I said, 'You don't know what you're talking about,'" Ms. Spencer says. "I slapped her."

While most of her classmates fretted over whether a boy would ask them for a date, Ms. Spencer worried about whether new acquaintances would grill her about her mother.

"I would never like to talk about it," Ms. Spencer says. "At first, I thought, 'What am I going to tell my friends? Are people not going to like me because my mother's in jail?' But my mother told me, 'Don't be afraid to admit that I am in the penitentiary. I'm not the only mother here.'"

"That helped," Ms. Spencer says. "That helped me a lot."

■ The friend

Eva Miles gave Joyce Ann Brown the black pin-striped suit she wore recently to a local radio talk show.

After Mrs. Brown left prison, Mrs. Miles gave her one other suit and a pair of gold earrings. While her friend was still behind bars, Mrs. Miles gave Mrs. Brown's daughter a stereo and a little money when she had extra to give.

Mrs. Miles also helped give the welcome-home party attended by 100 family members and friends. Weeks later, she gave a gospel concert and fashion sale to help raise money for the fledgling Joyce Ann Brown legal defense fund.

"I feel like Joyce was cheated out of nine years," Mrs. Miles says. "That I can't replace. I've had new dresses. New tennis shoes. That's the least she deserves."

Mrs. Brown says that Eva Miles is one of a handful of faithful friends who remembered her during the years she spent behind bars.

Mrs. Miles and Mrs. Brown met during the early '70s. The women shared a love of live blues and a penchant for hard partying.

"Every time Bobby Bland came to town, we'd go," Mrs. Miles remembers. "We never missed a show."

They cared for one another's children, a responsibility Mrs. Miles volunteered for full time shortly after Mrs. Brown's conviction.

"When Joyce first left, Koquice stayed with us for two to three months," Mrs. Miles says. "Her aunts would pick her up on weekends until her grandmother got everything situated."

When Koquice moved in with her grandparents, Eva Miles kept in touch with the family through phone calls. But she never visited her friend in the penitentiary.

"To tell you the truth, I never wanted to see her there," Mrs. Miles says. "I thought about our good times."

She also pondered the facts and the outcome of Mrs. Brown's case.

"In Texas," she says, "you're guilty until proven innocent. If it happened to her, it could happen to me. It could happen to anybody."

Mrs. Brown's conviction also changed her friend's lifestyle.

"I used to have a real bad temper," Mrs. Miles says. "I had an attitude. Not anymore. Now I'm also careful about who I associate with or where I go. All this has turned me into a real homebody. You can be doing what you're supposed to be doing and still have something bad like this happen."

▪ The accused

Joyce Ann Brown never imagined fighting with her mother over the proper preparation of a turkey dinner. But she and Ruby Kelley argued from 2:30 a.m. until 6 on Thanksgiving morning.

"She watched every move I made," says Mrs. Brown, who is 42. "I said, 'Girl, get out from under my heels and let me cook.' It was just like I was 11 or 12 and she was trying to teach me how to cook."

But to be anywhere near a home-cooked turkey dinner is a blessing; her previous nine Thanksgivings were spent in prison for a crime she swears she didn't commit.

Two weeks ago, she passed her driver's license exam with flying colors. These days, she is redecorating her sister Mary Black's bedroom suite. Mrs. Black and her husband moved out of that room and now sleep in bunks so that Mrs. Brown can have a private bath and a bigger bedroom.

She cares for her granddaughter, 3-year-old Brittany, and surrounds herself with friends and family. When she's alone, she writes the story of her life in a book she hopes to publish.

It is the dependence on family that she finds most limiting.

"I rely on my family for money," she says. "I don't like that. I'm not used to saying, 'May I borrow your car?' Sometimes I feel angry. I'm out here in the world, but I feel like I'm still in prison."

Joyce's defense team has never doubted her innocence.

"I'm not a bleeding heart, and people can't fool me," says Jack Strickland, one of her lawyers. "Most attorneys go their whole lives without being able to defend someone who is completely ... innocent. Joyce is innocent. Joyce is sincere."

That her charisma has struck a chord with the public amazes Mr. Strickland.

"I never had a client in my entire life who anyone wanted to touch, let alone hug," he says. "Joyce is different."

Mrs. Brown and her lawyers believe that her salvation had more to do with divine intervention than old-fashioned legal sleuthing.

"For years and years, I cried and wrote to everyone," Mrs. Brown says, "Everyone in the world can pray for you, but miracles happen when you pray for yourself."

Her prayers were answered by Centurion Ministries Inc. The agency was able to uncover evidence that led to the recent court ruling that freed Mrs. Brown.

"When I got on my knees to pray, people started coming into my life," says Mrs. Brown. "Positive people."

January 14, 1990

EPILOGUE: A month after this story appeared, the district attorney's office announced it would not retry Mrs. Brown's case. Soon afterward, she began her career as an administrative assistant to Dallas County Commissioner John Wiley Price. On Dec. 31, 1993, a state district judge expunged the charge of armed robbery from her record. Four months later, the former convict was appointed to a three-month term as assistant foreman of a Dallas County grand jury.

Invisible Men

■ ■ ■ ■ ■ ■ ■ ■ ■ ■

T he Rev. Willie C. Champion was preaching about AIDS. The disease, he shouted, was the wrath of God. The Lord, the pastor said, was using AIDS to punish gays and lesbians.

Parishioners said amen.

That was almost four years ago. Today, Dr. Champion preaches a different message to the members of his North Park Christian Methodist Episcopal Church. As a result, members of the Dallas church minister each week to gay men and others dying from AIDS.

"I went through a conversion experience," Dr. Champion says. "God had to change my heart."

Black gays and their advocates say the minister's transformation is welcome — as welcome as it is rare.

They say fear and hatred of gays are more intense among blacks than among whites. They say most blacks are so eager to deny the needs, or even the existence, of gay men that black gays are rendered almost invisible. They say that, although they can't prove it, they believe the isolation of black gays has contributed to the runaway increase of AIDS among black males.

"Homophobia is not, of course, unique to the black community, but it takes on a particular character within the context of African-American history and culture," writes Yale University associate law professor Harlon L. Dalton in an acclaimed essay titled "AIDS in Blackface." " ... In our denunciation of homosexuality and of persons thought to be gay, blacks (including closet gays) tend to be much more open and pointed than whites."

Dr. Champion's denunciations ended after an AIDS workshop, where he met a man whose keen intellect immediately impressed him. The two laughed and talked until it was time to take their seats. When the moderator introduced the participants, the minister discovered that his new friend had AIDS.

"I said, 'Oh, God,'" Dr. Champion says. "There I was, breathing the same air, shaking his hand. The Lord spoke to me. He said, 'Don't be afraid.' Right there, the Lord began to deal with my ignorance."

Although many blacks might prefer to ignore homosexuality in their midst, AIDS increasingly is forcing them to acknowledge it. Black gay and bisexual men have a rate of AIDS infection that is two to three times higher than their white counterparts', according to a 1988 report in the journal *American Psychologist*.

In "AIDS and the Law," Dr. Wayne L. Greaves writes that 70 percent of the AIDS patients treated at predominantly black Howard University Hospital in Washington during the late 1980s were homosexual.

"For some black parents, it is more acceptable to pretend that a son with AIDS was an intravenous drug user than to admit that he is gay," Dr. Greaves says in the book. "Yet the fact that nearly half of all black people with AIDS are gay or bisexual is a clear, if poignant, testament to their existence."

"We don't have gay men in the black community?" asks Reggie Williams, executive director of the National Task Force on AIDS Prevention. "Excuse me, but I've been here since day one, and I've been gay ever since."

'We don't have gay men in the black community? Excuse me, but I've been here since day one, and I've been gay ever since.'

■ ■ ■ ■ ■ ■ ■ ■ ■ ■ ■

Homophobia takes many forms, says Phill Wilson, AIDS coordinator for the city of Los Angeles and founder and co-chairman of the Black Lesbian and Gay Leadership Forum, a national group. Verbal taunts, physical abuse, job discrimination and self-imposed alienation are among its common manifestations.

At a Dallas support group for black, HIV-positive gay men, one man describes being beaten severely by his older brother, who objected to his homosexuality.

"He said, 'You're just a punk,'" James says. "My parents weren't there, so he beat the hell out of me. I guess it was just time to kick my ass, time to make a man out of me."

Ralph, a 36-year-old radiologist, says homophobia often forces gay black men to "live a lie." Like the other men who agreed to speak of their experiences, he does so only on the condition that his real name not be used. With cool detachment, he tells of being abandoned by his best childhood friend.

"When I came out to him, he freaked out on the spot," Ralph says. "He stopped speaking to me. That was years ago."

Ralph's family also had a hard time accepting him.

"Until three years ago," he says, "my mother was still trying to fix me up with a woman."

Damian, an architect, hosts a lavish Sunday brunch to introduce several men to a reporter who has agreed to guard their anonymity. He prepares six courses and flavored coffees and herbal teas. While waiting for guests to arrive, he fusses with the china and silver and nervously checks his watch.

"The churches are probably late today," he says.

The clock strikes 1:30.

"Mmmm," he says.

By 2:30, Damian is angry and embarrassed. "I invited 20 men," he says. "I can't believe no one even called."

Harold, a button-down radio producer, is surprised by Damian's surprise. *Paris is Burning*, a documentary about black gay transvestites, broke attendance records at a major New York City art house, drawing blacks and whites, straights and gays. Two recent Dallas screenings sold out, but failed to attract a significant black audience.

"Honeychile, straight blacks wouldn't dream of coming (to the film)," Harold says. "It's guilt by association."

"And gays, well, they want to keep their secret."

The roots of homophobia are difficult to unearth, says Mr. Dalton of Yale. Many black gays point to the black church. But Mr. Dalton is among black intellectuals who say blaming the church oversimplifies the issue.

124

In his analysis, blacks' hatred of homosexuality is more cultural than religious. Homosexuality is perceived as a threat to the survival of the black family, fragile since slavery, he says. In a culture where the pool of strong, effective husbands and fathers is already too small, homosexuality is thought to deplete the numbers further and reduce women's opportunities to be wives and mothers.

"Gay black men and lesbians are made to suffer because they are out of sync with a powerful cultural impulse to weaken black women and strengthen black men," Mr. Dalton writes. " ... My suspicion is that openly gay men and lesbians evoke hostility in part because they have come to symbolize the strong female and the weak male that slavery and Jim Crow produced."

Black gays also struggle to integrate three identities, says Ted Karpf, a Dallas-based AIDS specialist with the U.S. Department of Health and Human Services.

"Are they black first, male second, gay third?" Mr. Karpf asks. "Who knows? We do know that white men don't have to ask themselves whether they're being white."

And even if the church is not the birthplace of homophobia, it has sometimes appeared reluctant to address AIDS and other issues of concern to gays.

> **'Are they black first, male second, gay third? Who knows?'**
>
> ■ ■ ■ ■ ■ ■ ■ ■ ■ ■ ■

The Christian Methodist Episcopal church took the lead by organizing a seminar on AIDS for pastors in the Dallas area. Four hundred invitations were mailed to black churches. Five ministers showed up, Dr. Champion says.

"We were disappointed," he says.

Phil Matthews, director of minority outreach for the AIDS Interfaith Network Inc. of Dallas County, says black churches have been reluctant to address the disease because many congregations have too little money or are overburdened with other social concerns. In addition, says Mr. Matthews, an ordained minister and a graduate of Southern Methodist University's Perkins School of Theology, many are bound by literal interpretations of the Scripture that condemn homosexuality.

But Harold, who is a lapsed Baptist, argues that many religious taboos, what he calls the "shall nots," reflect human prejudices rather than divine directives.

"In my lifetime, I remember ministers preaching from the pulpit that God wanted segregation," he says angrily. "Black churches are doing what Southern white churches did 30 years ago. The Bible says as much of nothing about homosexuality as it did about integration and the mixing of races."

A number of black gays attend traditional churches but keep their sexuality a secret, Dr. Champion says.

"There have always been homosexuals in the black church," he says. "The pulpit is not immune to homosexuality. They are our musicians and singers. They're on the usher boards and in the singles ministries."

'They are our musicians and singers. They're on the usher boards and in the singles ministries.'

▪ ▪ ▪ ▪ ▪ ▪ ▪ ▪ ▪ ▪ ▪

Black ministers don't welcome openly gay members, though, because straight parishioners would criticize them for condoning homosexuality, Dr. Champion says. "We haven't allowed ourselves to become educated. It's easier to ignore or condemn them than to deal with the issues.

"When we deal with AIDS, we have to deal with drug abuse," Dr. Champion says. "We've got to deal with sex. Sex is an area we in the black church have problems with. The only way we have of dealing is by telling people no."

Ralph, whose father is a Pentecostal pastor, says that after he came out, he was forced to quit the usher board, choir and youth ministry at his West Dallas church.

"I couldn't just sit there and be a 'bench member,'" Ralph says. "I left."

The consequences of homophobia are many, says Alpha Thomas, an AIDS educator with the Dallas Urban League. She points to the refusal to use condoms as evidence that isolation and despair have made black gays fatalistic.

126

In the first study of attitudes and sexual behavior among black gay men, conducted last year in 23 U.S. cities, researchers found that 46.5 percent engaged in unprotected sex, though most were well informed. This is more than two times the figure for unprotected sex among the overall adult gay population, according to a 1990 study by the federal Centers for Disease Control and the National Association of Black and White Men Together.

In April, U.S. Health and Human Services Director Louis W. Sullivan reported that AIDS and rising homicide rates have reduced the average lifespan of black men to 64.9 years, 7.4 years shorter than that of white men.

"I know men whose lovers have died of AIDS, and they still won't use condoms," Ms. Thomas says. "I know there's no proof, but I talk with these men. I think a lot of these men feel unloved by their families, so they look for affection in multiple sex partners."

"Why suffer or sacrifice in the short run when I can have it all now?" asks Harold. "Our lives are so finite, anyway."

Michael, a 28-year-old librarian who was discharged from the military after he tested positive for the HIV virus, continued to have unprotected sex.

"What do those military quacks know?" he asks.

Over two years, Michael took the test twice more, accepting his condition only after the third test came back positive.

Fear and denial also prompt many black gays to "pass" as straight, just as many light-complexioned blacks once passed as white. Several men report that they have refused to speak up against discrimination and even have married to avoid disclosure.

"You have to play games with yourself all the time," says Freeman, a Methodist minister. "I'm tolerated as long as I'm silent and inconspicuous. If only I was not black and not gay. Both have caused me so much isolation."

A number of black gays say they despise the "bootie" jokes told by comedian Eddie Murphy, but most refuse to object publicly for fear of being labeled gay. Privately, some also criticize popular Dallas radio announcer Tom Joyner.

In one of the DJ's long-running gags, he lampoons a black drag queen. The imaginary character, Brucie, The Rib Fairy, drives a pink

Cadillac, dresses in hot pants, a halter top and heels, and sneaks slabs of ribs to deserving picnickers during summer holidays.

Mr. Joyner expresses surprise that gay listeners find this and other jokes derogatory.

"Really?" he asks. "To tell you the truth, I've been doing these routines for 10 years. In 10 years, I received just one, anonymous complaint.

"When you do comedy, you run the risk of offending someone," he says. "If they say I'm insensitive, then I guess I'm insensitive. I'm really sorry. I don't harbor any ill will toward gay people. I don't hate gays."

Efforts to "pass" can have deadly implications when gay men marry and then have unprotected sex with their wives and with other men.

Although few figures are available, the 1990 survey found that one-third of the respondents reported having sex with both men and women. Black women are 4.6 times more likely to contract AIDS from a bisexual man than are white women, according to a 1988 *American Journal of Public Health* article.

Ralph, divorced after two years, says he married because friends and family expected him to. He begins to count on his fingers the married gay men he knows. When he reaches 10, he says, "Hell, I hardly know anybody who hasn't been married."

James, father of a 14-year-old son, says that though he briefly stopped picking up men after he married, his attraction to his own sex didn't end, as he hoped it would.

"I could barely fight that battle," he says. "One day my wife asked, 'Are you gay?' I wasn't strong enough to say yes."

June 23, 1991

Empty Places

∎∎∎∎∎∎∎∎∎∎

very weekday morning, Angela Johnson rises at 4:30, nearly two hours earlier than she did before the Persian Gulf War. She uses the extra hours to feed her three daughters and drive them to school. Her husband handled those tasks — until he was sent to Saudi Arabia.

As an activated Marine reservist, Sgt. Alfred Johnson, 35, delivers supplies to the front lines. At home in Dallas, he also delivered — whatever he promised and a lot that he didn't.

Like many of the men and women stationed in the Persian Gulf, Mr. Johnson is a loving spouse and a doting parent. His absence has left gaps in the lives of his family. But it also has created unexpected voids in the lives of others with whom he came into regular contact — the watch repairman and the bank teller, the brother-in-law and the business partner.

To friends, he is the man who would listen and pray with them in times of trouble. To members of his church, he is the Rev. Alfred Johnson, the junior pastor who preached so long that his wife often signaled him to stop with a sharp glance at her watch. To colleagues and clients, he is a reliable computer technician. To his mother and father, he is a dependable son.

His story is important not because he is a hero, but because he is an ordinary, good man — much like the others who serve with him.

∎∎∎∎∎∎∎∎∎∎

His story is important not because he is a hero, but because he is an ordinary, good man — much like the half-million other men and women who serve with him. Every one of those 500,000 Alfred Johnsons brings the pain of war home to those helped by their presence and touched by their absence.

▪ A watch for the war

Alfred Johnson is wearing Jimmy Williams' favorite watch, a black Casio specially designed for deep-sea divers.

Just days before he was deployed, Mr. Johnson stopped by Jimmy's Watch Repair Shop to collect the Seiko he'd left for service. It wasn't ready.

The two men talked as they had nearly every week since the day six months ago when Mr. Johnson first came in for a repair.

They hit it off then, and Mr. Johnson began stopping by regularly. Mr. Williams says Mr. Johnson always managed to engage him in provocative discussions about County Commissioner John Wiley Price, economic instability in South Dallas, public schools and a host of other issues.

"He really surprised me with his knowledge of Dallas politics and stuff like that," says Mr. Williams, 45. "Young men his age usually don't talk about that kind of thing."

During that last visit, Mr. Johnson seemed distracted.

"We talked 40, maybe 45, minutes," Mr. Williams says. "He seemed a little tense about the war."

Finally, Mr. Johnson asked if his watch would be ready the next day. "He said, 'I really need my watch, I'm shipping out,'" Mr. Williams recalls. "Really, I didn't know he was going over there."

Mr. Williams gets quiet for a minute.

"I took the watch off my arm and gave it to him," he says. "He was really surprised.

"He needed a watch," Mr. Williams says. "Besides, this guy was going over there to do something for me, for this country."

▪ The dependable son

Lena Johnson turns up the volume on her living-room television set before she goes to the kitchen to cook. She slides the volume even higher before going to scrub the bathroom. Each night, she falls asleep listening to the TV, its blue light throwing shadows on the walls of her little Dallas house.

"Now I sit and watch the TV and listen for them to say the war is over, and he is coming home," she says of her son the Marine.

Mrs. Johnson, 63, and her husband, Selery, 82, need their son. As a child, Alfred depended on them. The last year or so, they've come to count on him.

"I turned to Alfred because he's real strong," says Mrs. Johnson, plucking a portrait of her son from the living room wall. "No matter how many kids you got, one always seems to be more dependable."

When there wasn't enough left from the Johnsons' Social Security checks, Alfred would pay his parents' bills.

"I got past due notices this morning," says Mrs. Johnson, pulling a small pile of envelopes from her purse.

When their sink clogged, he would drive over from his suburban Dallas home to fix it. If their old car sprang a flat, he would repair it before the sun set.

"My husband has heart trouble," says Mrs. Johnson, "and he can't hardly do much. If his daddy had to go anywhere, Alfred would come on over and take him."

Parents of six girls and five boys, the Johnsons have experienced many tragedies. One son was murdered a decade ago. Three years ago, another son was killed in a car accident. Another rarely visits, and the youngest is serving a prison sentence in Arkansas.

'He was the only one who would sit down here and talk to me about the Bible.'

■ ■ ■ ■ ■ ■ ■ ■ ■ ■

"The girls do the best they can," Mrs. Johnson says. "But they got their own families now. They're trying hard to make it."

Alfred, however, was always there. "We had good conversations about the Bible," Mrs. Johnson says. "He was the only one who would sit down here and talk to me about the Bible."

These days, deep furrows crease the mother's brow. Her brown eyes dart nervously, and she wrings her plump hands.

It's hard, she says, to feel patriotic about Alfred's serving his country. "I just think I'm one person who has had it."

▪ Not just any technician

Alfred Johnson didn't need a degree in computer science to become a computer expert. His formal education ended when he graduated from Pinkston High School in 1974.

But four years ago, when IBM hired him to assemble computers, it was as if he'd been born knowing how to make the machines work, says Clarence Edwards, a programmer who has worked at the company for 19 years.

"You can go to any technician to get things done," Mr. Edwards says. "But to get them done right the first time, you had to go to Alfred."

Mr. Johnson quickly moved from building computers to troubleshooting them and teaching others to use them.

"He is a gifted teacher," Mr. Edwards says. "He was always very enthusiastic when people caught on to what he was showing them.... He said, 'I can't believe you guys are using this so fast.'"

Mr. Edwards was so impressed by Mr. Johnson's abilities that he became his part-time business partner when Mr. Johnson decided to leave IBM and open his own computer service business last year.

"I helped him with contract negotiations and with securing financing," Mr. Edwards says.

But just as business began to pick up, Marine Sgt. Johnson was deployed to Saudi Arabia.

▪ Praying for Daddy

Katrina, Brittney and Shante Johnson miss their daddy's homemade breakfasts. Listlessly, they slide stacks of microwave pancakes around on their plates.

"He'd make scratch, old-fashioned pancakes for them," says Angela Johnson, 34, an IBM procurement assistant. "I don't have time for that."

She tries her best to keep her husband's absence from causing too much strain in the little girls' lives. But she can't stop them from missing him and worrying about him.

At 11 months, Shante is the least affected.

But 2-year-old Brittney cried a lot at first, Mrs. Johnson says.

"Every time the phone rang, she thought it was Daddy. When the doorbell rang, she thought it was Daddy. When she woke up last night, she cried for Daddy."

At school, a teacher noticed that 7-year-old Katrina stood by silently while other students played kickball.

"She was kind of distant, so I asked her what was the matter," says the teacher, Gardellia Walton. "She said she missed her daddy, so I took her inside.

"I told her, 'The next time you write your daddy, encourage him — tell him we're all praying for his safe return.'"

Katrina did write a letter.

"I wrote, 'Daddy, I miss you,'" she says. "'I wish you would come home. I pray for you, Daddy — that you won't die.'"

■ A right-hand man

There's an empty chair behind the pulpit at Believers in Christ Christian Center. Sgt. Alfred Johnson, known to the congregation as the Rev. Alfred Johnson, sat there during every service.

The young co-pastor devoted most of his free time to the little church. His commitment freed the senior minister, the Rev. T.W. Grimes, to pursue a multitude of community service projects.

"Every pastor needs a right-hand man," says Mr. Grimes, who is Angela Johnson's brother. "I feel like mine has been taken away from me."

Mr. Johnson opened the church building and began the Friday midnight prayer services.

He organized other prayer meetings and often picked up congregation members who needed rides to church, the grocery store or the doctor's office.

"When we have brotherhood meetings, he would be the one to get together the barbecue pit," Mr. Grimes says.

"His favorite question was, 'What do you want me to do?'"

■ Finding common ground

Alfred Johnson walked into H.D. Johnson's Lewisville law office one night about two years ago.

"I tend to work late," H.D. says. "He saw the light on and just dropped in."

H.D., executive director of U.S. Arbitration & Mediation-Southwest, is white. Alfred is black. Despite their different backgrounds, the men became fast friends.

"Alfred is a very unusual man," H.D. says. "I get the feeling that with Alfred, what you see is what you get. He has no guile. He's almost innocent."

They found common ground in computers, their shared passion.

Alfred had spotted a computer on H.D.'s desk and soon started troubleshooting problems with the lawyer's office system.

"He and I have spent many a night in the office with bits and pieces of computers spread across the rug, trying to figure out the problem," H.D. says. "He saved me a lot of money."

Last spring, H.D. became one of Alfred's first customers.

"He's one of those guys you can call at 5 o'clock on a Friday night, and he'll be here in the hour and work till 10 to get it done," H.D. says. "He has a tremendous amount of drive."

Alfred's deployment surprised H.D.

"I walked into my office one morning and found on my desk a piece of software we'd been talking about," H.D. says. "The note said his reserve unit had been called up."

H.D. says his friend's departure has left a void.

"First, we're friends," H.D. says. "Second, I'm a client. Since he left, I haven't had anybody to bounce new ideas off of. I can find another computer consultant, but I can't find another Sir Alfred."

■ A troubled boy disappears

No one has seen Mark since Alfred Johnson was deployed to Operation Desert Storm.

"The week after Rev. Johnson left, he just went poof," says Mr. Grimes, the senior pastor.

134

The 16-year-old boy had been shuffled from foster home to foster home until Mr. Grimes persuaded Alfred and Angela Johnson to become his guardians eight months ago.

"We try to help people," Mrs. Johnson says. "You never know when you'll need a hand."

At first, Mark was very shy.

"He had to adjust to the rules and regulations of our household," Mrs. Johnson says. "He'd never lived with a male authority figure. He never had anyone tell him what to do, so he was very quiet until he got used to Al."

Soon, however, he seemed happy, and the girls told people he was their big brother. Mrs. Johnson says the hardest thing she has had to tell her husband since his departure was that Mark had disappeared.

Even now, she can hardly talk about "the situation," as she calls it. "It's really kind of hurt me that he left as soon as Al left," she says, her voice beginning to break. "We opened our home to him, and our families accepted him as part of us. It's an unfortunate situation. I'm still trying to get over it myself."

The news that Mr. Johnson would be leaving apparently stirred up Mark's old anger and insecurities, says Dorothy Johnson, one of Mr. Johnson's sisters.

"Mark started rejecting Al when he found out he was going to Saudi Arabia," Dorothy Johnson says. "I guess the boy felt rejected again."

Lena Johnson, Alfred's mother, says the man and boy had become as close as father and son. "Every time Al came to visit, Mark followed right behind him," she says. "Mark called Al 'Daddy.'"

February 10, 1991

SECTION VI

·

ANCESTRAL

VOICES

··········

A Brush
With Destiny

■ ■ ■ ■ ■ ■ ■ ■ ■ ■

ois Mailou Jones stood staring at the painting so long that an art museum guard walked over and started a conversation. "You must love art," he said. "Yes," she said, "I do." She wanted to tell the truth. She wanted to say the piece that held her gaze was her own. That a white friend had submitted it to the exhibition. That the guard and everyone else ought to know her work was good enough to hang in mainstream museums and galleries.

But Ms. Jones kept quiet. She loathed having her friend accused of deception. She feared having her work rejected. And in the 1930s, when the incident occurred, black men and women routinely were denied a public persona no matter how talented they might be.

"It was terribly disheartening," Ms. Jones says. "It was impossible to get into shows. Curators and gallery owners would say, 'You're a Negro. We can't handle your work.' My work was always hung," she says quietly, "but no one knew Lois Jones was black."

'Curators and gallery owners would say, "You're a Negro. We can't handle your work." '

■ ■ ■ ■ ■ ■ ■ ■ ■ ■

No trace of bitterness creeps into her voice as she shares this anecdote — one of hundreds that mark the 87-year-old artist's exhilarating, fulfilling and sometimes heartbreaking journey from obscurity to renown. Ms. Jones tells her story during a break from a round of celebrations held to honor the Dallas opening of "The World of Lois Mailou Jones," a 3-year-old traveling retrospective of her art.

Six decades after Ms. Jones sneaked her pieces into exhibitions, critics, historians and the general public can't get enough of the vinegary octogenarian and her art. Hampton University and actor Danny Glover are in a bidding war over *Mediation (Mob Victim)*, a 1944 painting that hauntingly depicts a lynching victim. Major museums and galleries are collecting pieces from Ms. Jones' retrospective. Requests for the exhibit flow into the exhibit organizers' Washington offices. And high attendance has led to extensions of up to several weeks in several cities.

The Jones phenomenon has startled and pleased the show's organizer, Meridian House International, a nonprofit Washington agency that uses art and culture to promote international cooperation. "Our traveling exhibition program began with Lois," says Nancy Matthews, spokeswoman for Meridian House. "It's just been a tremendous success."

Meridian House isn't far from Ms. Jones' Washington home. It isn't that far from Howard University, where Ms. Jones taught art for 47 years. But Ms. Matthews had never heard anyone utter Ms. Jones' name. Then in 1989, an Ethiopian artist visiting Meridian House asked the staff to find Ms. Jones, whom he had met when she visited Africa in the 1970s. Ms. Matthews invited Ms. Jones to a dinner party she hosted for the Ethiopian visitor. The women hit it off, and Ms. Jones invited Ms. Matthews to see her work.

"She was wonderful. Her work was wonderful," Ms. Matthews says. "I thought, 'This woman should have a show in Washington.' A year later, "The World of Lois Mailou Jones" opened at Meridian House. "Her students came from all over the country," Ms. Matthews says. "It had to be extended twice."

Part of the draw is Ms. Jones herself. An eloquent raconteur with stylish presence, she speaks at most of the exhibit's openings. "Although the talks have taken me out of my studio, I enjoy meeting all these people," she says. "Twenty-five years ago, I was so discouraged. I was ready for this kind of acclaim 55 years ago."

Decade after decade, recognition eluded her. Rather than mount an individual battle against discrimination, she chose to concentrate on her art. She painted most evenings and each weekend, trying a variety of styles and media.

A native of Boston, Ms. Jones traces her earliest artistic efforts to age 7, when her parents gave her a paint set to take on vacation. At Martha's Vineyard, where her family spent summers, she dabbled in landscapes.

"We lived in a smoky apartment on the top floor of a building across from the Boston City Hall," she says. "Something happened to me at the Vineyard. I think it was the blue of the water and the hillsides of buttercups and daisies."

She won admission to some of the country's most prestigious art schools and designed textiles after graduation. Although her fabrics appeared on sofas, pillows and other home furnishings, she found design thankless and frustrating. "My signature appeared on nothing," she says. "I couldn't take credit for anything."

Meta Warwick Fuller, an acclaimed black sculptor, advised Ms. Jones to leave the United States. "She said, 'You're talented but you won't be successful in this country.'"

So Ms. Jones joined the scores of black expatriates in Paris and enjoyed unprecedented recognition when her professors entered her art in competitions and shows. "My work was accepted by galleries," she recalls. "I could eat anywhere I wanted. I could move about freely. The French people love black Americans."

'My signature appeared on nothing. I couldn't take credit for anything.'

■ ■ ■ ■ ■ ■ ■ ■ ■ ■

Her French experience strengthened her for what she would endure once she returned to the United States in the early 1940s. "I knew I had talent," she says. "I was written up in the *Beaux Arts Journal*. That helped me overcome any bitterness."

Alain Locke, the late American philosopher and cultural critic, admonished Ms. Jones to incorporate African and African-American themes into her work, which was heavily influenced by her classic European training. "He said, 'Look at what Matisse and Modigliani and Picasso are doing to African art,'" she says. "'Africa is part of your heritage, not theirs.'"

The bright colors, spiritual and secular iconography and planar designs found in Ms. Jones' recent work are markedly different from the impressionistic style she often used in her earlier works. The exhibit offers samples from several periods of her career: academic exercises, oils, watercolors, pieces painted in France and art resulting from her exposure to Haitian and African cultures.

Her broad experimentation makes her work difficult to categorize, but she never intended to evoke a singular style or era. Her challenge, she says, was to be recognized as an American artist. "That's what I wanted," she says, laughing. "I'm a terrible old Scorpio. We're a very tenacious people."

Ms. Jones considers her friendship with the late television newsman Max Robinson among her most influential relationships. Mr. Robinson painted and collected the works of African-American artists. She sold eight pieces to him only after he agreed to donate them to museums, rather than sell or bequeath them. "After all these years," she says, shaking her head, museums and galleries don't collect black artists with any enthusiasm or seriousness. "They want private collectors to donate our work."

Mr. Robinson's contributions to the National Portrait Gallery in Washington and to the Metropolitan Museum of Art in New York have enabled her to stand before her work and claim it as her own. "I said, 'I've made it,'" she says. "This exhibit is the icing on the cake."

June 19, 1993

Sanctuary

■ ■ ■ ■ ■ ■ ■ ■ ■ ■

PARIS — For James A. Emanuel, America is a memory. It is sometimes pleasant — the thump of his feet whacking the pavement during a grade-school race; or sometimes painful — the tragic death of his only child. But a memory just the same.

"I have no plans to go back," he says quietly. "You're supposed to run away from the devil. You're supposed to run away from things that are killing you."

Since the late 19th century, declarations to that effect have been made by disillusioned African-American artists seeking sanctuary on the eastern shores of the North Atlantic. Individual artists and small enclaves settled in cities in Spain, England, Italy, Germany, Denmark, Russia and France. Especially Paris, where the tradition was honored during the recent "African Americans and Europe" conference.

A product of that history, Dr. Emanuel remains one of the few to uphold the tradition, says Michel Fabre, founding director of the Centre D'Etudes Afro-americaines at the Universite de la Sorbonne Nouvelle in Paris. "There are some black Americans working here," Dr. Fabre says. "I believe it's not a community in the sense it once was. I'm not sure it's considerable in terms of sheer numbers. What I feel is that for black artists now, it is a little easier to get recognition in America."

'You're supposed to run away from the devil. You're supposed to run away from things that are killing you.'

■ ■ ■ ■ ■ ■ ■ ■ ■ ■

Dr. Emanuel, a pioneer in the study of black literature and a critically acclaimed poet, is a living link to past expatriates, says Princeton University literary scholar Arnold Rampersad — "from Hughes to Baldwin, to Wright to Hemingway and others who came before them." For Dr. Emanuel and other African Americans, changes in the United States came long after they discovered the Old World and found it more humane.

"If I'm hungry, I want food right now," Dr. Emanuel says. "There is something hypocritical about supplying someone with something when their need is gone. It's too late for me."

Dr. Emanuel selects his words carefully, as if explaining philosophy in the classroom rather than chatting after breakfast in his three-room apartment. Except for gentle hand gestures, he sits still as he recalls the events that led him to this silent flat five stories above bustling Boulevard du Montparnasse. "To me it seems like eight months rather than eight years," Dr. Emanuel says. "I've been busy."

His journey ended in Paris after a lifetime of extended visits to southern France, Poland, England and Africa. Offers to teach flooded in after his landmark 1967 publication of *Langston Hughes*, a critical analysis of the poet's work, and *Dark Symphony: Negro Literature in America,* an exhaustive 1968 anthology he co-edited.

A series of prestigious overseas teaching assignments may have stimulated Dr. Emanuel's fondness for foreign countries, says Jerome Brooks, a former colleague who met the poet and scholar at City University of New York during the mid-1960s. "He availed himself of these (opportunities) liberally," adding more than six years of international teaching to his lengthy resume, says Dr. Brooks. A particularly prolific stay in London, in 1978, convinced Dr. Emanuel that America — and New York, in particular — ranked among his least supportive environments. He left London and spent the next three years in France.

"In New York, I couldn't write," Dr. Emanuel says. "In London, I did nothing but write day and night. I would just run up the stairs to my flat. I knew I didn't have anything to do but write."

He returned to New York in 1981 and struggled to balance poetry, teaching and personal responsibilities. As he inched toward retirement, academia grew tiring, less interesting and ultimately, unchallenging. His thirst for scholarship slowly evaporated. "I actually enjoyed teaching very much," he says. "But I don't go backwards unless I'm dragged backwards."

The feelings weren't new. His attentions first swayed from scholarship when he poured his analytical energies into the groundbreaking books on Langston Hughes and black literature. He ended his career as a critic abruptly, in the mid-1970s, after publishing some 30 articles of criticism, and having established the study of African-American literature as a legitimate academic discipline. That done, he concentrated on teaching and crafting poems.

"By that time, young, smart black scholars were beginning to write about black literature," Dr. Emanuel says. "I wasn't needed anymore. I switched to my love, poetry."

What the scholar/poet had achieved in criticism was pioneering, says Dr. Rampersad. The author of a 1989 Pulitzer Prize finalist, *The Life of Langston Hughes, Vol. II 1941-1967: I Dream A World,* remains reverent.

"There were no courses in African-American literature when Emanuel started out," Dr. Rampersad says. "He researched everything from the original texts." What most impressed Dr. Rampersad was that Dr. Emanuel managed to publish an error-free volume on Mr. Hughes. "My book had mistakes," Dr. Rampersad says. "His didn't."

'I don't go backwards unless I'm dragged backwards.'

■ ■ ■ ■ ■ ■ ■ ■ ■ ■

Confronting racism Dr. Emanuel was never able to enjoy fully the accolades, the appreciation, the recognition. Socially conscious, he attempted to confront racism — in his poetry and in his life. He launched an unsuccessful 1966 campaign for a school board seat in Mount Vernon, a New York City suburb. He recorded the experience and paid tribute to the district's children in his poem *To the Negro Children of Mount Vernon (On the Occasion of My School Board Candidacy).*

"Langston Hughes told me I was lucky I lost," Dr. Emanuel says.

His positions on controversial issues, such as integration in the early '60s, created a host of unexpected problems. "People ignored me," Dr. Emanuel says. "My car was sabotaged. I couldn't get repair people to come to my home ... all because I wanted black children to have an equal education."

Dr. Brooks says that while his former colleague and mentor maintained a quiet dignity during the turbulent '60s, fury trickled into Dr. Emanuel's poems. "Jim always had an awareness of the political realities," Dr. Brooks says. "I always sensed that he was shocked by political life, though. He carried the burden of being the first black faculty member here.

"Most of Jim's poems are not about his anger at all," Dr. Brooks adds. "There is always a lot of love, even sexiness in his work. On another level, there is a tremendous anger right beneath the surface."

A wave of sadness creeps into Dr. Emanuel's voice at the mention of Emmett Till's name.

▪ ▪ ▪ ▪ ▪ ▪ ▪ ▪ ▪ ▪

His anger and pain surfaces in "Afro-America, The Garden," a chapter of 42 poems appearing in *Whole Grain: Collected Poems: 1958-1989* (Lotus Press). The section's poems address poverty, police brutality, bigotry and actual events, such as the 1955 drowning of Emmett Till, a teen-age boy murdered in Mississippi by local people who claimed that he had insulted a white woman.

A wave of sadness creeps into Dr. Emanuel's voice at the mention of the dead teenager's name. "The fact that he was murdered is a disgrace," says Dr. Emanuel, nodding. "The fact that there is any racism at all continues to be a disgrace."

He says that although he isn't oblivious to growing debates about racial strife in France, it doesn't affect him. "In Paris, I don't feel racism," Dr. Emanuel says. "I hear about it on the radio here, but it doesn't hurt my feelings. It doesn't hurt my soul. Here, I'm an alien."

Like Mr. Hughes, James Baldwin, Richard Wright and others, Dr. Emanuel has endured significant personal tragedies — events that may have hastened his permanent move to Europe, says Dr.

Rampersad. Besides a particularly bitter divorce, the poet lost his only son, James Jr., in 1983.

Dr. Emanuel says his son, who was 29, protested when police officers arrested him for sleeping in a California park. He resisted arrest and was severely beaten. After he was released from jail, Dr. Emanuel says, officers continued to harass James Jr., and he grew increasingly despondent. Eventually, he shot himself.

"What happened was worse than if they had killed him," Dr. Emanuel says. "It shows what despair can drive a person to. It says more about racism's virulence than any other event I have known." The poet refuses to detail the incidents, but remains convinced that his son was a victim of police brutality. Those feelings are described in the poem *Deadly James (For All the Victims of Police Brutality),* in a 1987 collection published by Lotus Press.

Although he didn't know a soul in the city, he purchased the Paris apartment less than a year after burying his only child. His home is in the district of historic cafes once frequented by Simone de Beauvoir, Jean Paul Sartre, Henri Matisse, Marc Chagall and dozens of African-American artists.

"Everyone gets a wound that won't heal," he explains. "None of us ran away. "You 'run away' if it is your ethical, moral and practical obligation to stay," Dr. Emanuel says. "A man breaks a higher moral ground when he stays in an atmosphere that poisons him spiritually. Man has a responsibility to protect what is good in him."

The move has done him good, says Naomi Long Madgett, Dr. Emanuel's longtime editor at Lotus Press. "I never felt he was forced to leave, but being out of the situation that we've been in in this country must free him somewhat," she says. "His life seems to be so unencumbered now. Some of his poetry had drifted away from the lyricism that I liked better in the earlier poems. I think he's coming back to it."

While living in France, Dr. Emanuel has learned restaurant French. He spends most of his time alone, writing and reading. He fills his free time with long walks, household chores and conferring with his illustrator, Keith O. Anderson, a fellow expatriate. "I sleep eight hours," Dr. Emanuel says. "It enables me to keep active. I have no business being tired."

One of his favorite chores, he says, is hand-washing his clothes. "I use a plunger," he says. "It sucks the soap and water through my clothes." He says his life is exciting "in the way that writing poetry is exciting."

He prefers the almost absolute isolation that Paris provides. His address and phone number are not listed in local directories. "Isolation is good for me," he says. "My life is interior."

Dr. Emanuel's sister, Julie Williams of Denver, also says solitude suits her brother's pensive nature. Their mother, the late Cora Ann Emanuel, was a Christian Scientist who would make her seven children sit silently for a half-hour each day. The children were instructed to read a book or draw a picture. Dr. Emanuel read.

"There was a pile of books in his room," Mrs. Williams says. "He defied anyone to go in and touch them. He would just have a fit."

Books remain his prized possessions. They dominate his little apartment. Books by D.H. Lawrence and Hemingway sit next to volume after volume of literary criticism and collections of poetry. Short stacks of books totter on the little folding table that substitutes for a desk. His own books — 11, including 1991's *Whole Grain* — are piled to the ceiling of a narrow white closet. Life is just the way he needs it.

"Up here, in Paris, it's very quiet," he says. "There's not a sound."

March 15, 1992

500 Americans in Paris

■ ■ ■ ■ ■ ■ ■ ■ ■ ■

PARIS — Michel Fabre had an intimate thing in mind. He'd gather 100 pre-eminent scholars in Paris to discuss the impact Europe has had on African-American literature. That was early last summer. By fall, few lovers of African-American culture and arts didn't know about the exclusive event.

Scholars contacted by Dr. Fabre told their students, who invited their friends. Then someone told writers, who told visual artists, who invited musicians. Before organizers knew it, nearly 500 scholars, students and artists from 20 countries had registered for the February conference, "African Americans and Europe," the first such gathering since 1956.

"The registrations and phone calls just kept coming," says Dr. Fabre. "It got me very filled with anxiety, but I felt better knowing that whatever happened here would be important in people's lives."

Princeton University professor Arnold Rampersad, award-winning biographer of the poet Langston Hughes, sensed a desire for this type of conference long before it was proposed. "There was a feeling of almost palpable hunger on the part of African Americans for this to happen," he says.

And happen it did. Sponsorship from Harvard, Columbia, the University of Mississippi and the Centre d'Etudes Afro-americaines de la Sorbonne Nouvelle provided five

> 'There was a feeling of almost palpable hunger on the part of African Americans for this to happen.'

■ ■ ■ ■ ■ ■ ■ ■ ■ ■

149

full days of concurrent sessions on literature, music, film and visual arts. The presentations stirred debate, drew chuckles and caused tears. Panels such as "The USSR and African Americans," "Painters and Sculptors and Ideology," "Realities of Racism in Europe" and "Music and Performance" attracted enthusiastic listeners to seminar rooms at the Sorbonne, the Palais du Luxembourg, the Images d'Ailleurs and other locations that offered free and ample space.

The "vibe," as participants called the conference's air of excitement, came close to replicating the days when scholars descended on Paris to exchange thoughts, says Dr. Fabre, a Richard Wright scholar and founding director of the Centre d'Etudes Afro-americaines. It also gave the French much to muse about.

"Europe is a place where your writers and artists were recognized simply because they should have been," Dr. Fabre says. "This program is a celebration of black American culture, and it is a way of saying to the people of France that the black experience is not only essential to American culture but to our culture also."

They talked about James Baldwin, Josephine Baker, Richard Wright and Thelonious Monk.

■ ■ ■ ■ ■ ■ ■ ■ ■ ■

Small waves of black American artists and intellectuals began migrating to Europe before the turn of the century. Their population soared immediately after World War II, when veterans, enamored of their social acceptance and hero status, used the then-new GI Bill to study at European universities, start businesses and settle. More than a hundred years of this history gave participants enough subjects to talk about deep into the night.

And talk they did. About James Baldwin, who wrote *Another Country* while living in Paris. About Josephine Baker, the toast of Paris' cafe society. About Thelonious Monk and Charlie Parker, who wrote some of their most memorable jazz here. And Richard Wright, the enigmatic writer and French hero.

Celebrated children's writer Mildred Pitts Walter of Denver says she especially appreciated the chance to hear about her favorite writers' personal lives. "The best part was listening to Richard Wright's daughter and getting a perspective from the eyes of his child," Ms. Walter says. "She saw him as a human being. That was a nice change from the usual stories."

Participants, mostly African-American scholars and artists, also discussed their own days in Europe. Visual artists huddled like schoolboys and loudly proclaimed plans to meet for drinks after the day's panels. Big and little parties provided venues for continued discussions and good-spirited divisions.

"The artists seemed intent on doing their own thing," says Ms. Walter, author of 14 books. "A lot of people who couldn't get to the writers' parties went to the artists' parties." Or to the ongoing film festival. Or to the plays and performance-art pieces. Or to the jazz concerts.

Writers, who with scholars dominated the conference, held court all over Paris. There were official conference-organized readings, impromptu writer-organized readings and a "marathon" reading for anyone who felt he or she had written something someone might want to hear. More than a dozen poets, essayists and fiction writers hauled copies of their books to Paris, making conference headquarters resemble sale tables at the local B. Dalton Booksellers.

Schmoozing reached new heights in the halls outside of the sessions. Even the panel discussions were joyfully interrupted by pitched whispers as surprised professors and former students greeted one another. "I liked seeing a lot of people I hadn't seen in a long time," says Joyce Marie Jackson, a professor of ethno-musicology at Louisiana State University. "I ran into people I went to school with. It was fun to meet up in Paris."

The French, often accused of being xenophobic, seemed to welcome this temporary invasion. A dozen bookstores near the conference sites displayed books and art reflecting the African-American experience. Innkeepers were especially benevolent about bad pronunciation, and taxi drivers patiently figured out where people needed to go.

Galerie d'Art Noir Contemporain and Galerie Resche opened exhibits of works by expatriate visual artists during the conference. Art lovers ignored the cold winter air and spilled into the streets surrounding the galleries. Aaron "Sharp" Goodstone, a New York-born abstract artist, couldn't squeeze inside to watch people admiring his work. "This is amazing, man," says Mr. Goodstone. "I couldn't get Americans to pay much attention to my work when I lived there."

A California film crew lent an air of glamour to the conference. The crew accompanied Asake Bomani, who is co-producing a documentary about expatriate visual artists. Everyone seemed to adore her. Screams of "Asake!" were heard all over the conference. Ms. Bomani, wife of actor Danny Glover, owns a hip San Francisco gallery. Bomani Gallery is exhibiting "Paris Connections," a retrospective of works by African-American visual artists who worked and still work in Paris. Mr. Glover attended the conference, too, popping up at sessions on the Harlem Renaissance.

'This is amazing, man. I couldn't get Americans to pay much attention to my work ...'

■ ■ ■ ■ ■ ■ ■ ■ ■ ■

That touch of Hollywood notwithstanding, the real stars were the writers and visual artists, says Gordon Thompson, assistant professor of English at City University of New York. The Yale-trained scholar says his early favorite was novelist Paule Marshall, who delighted participants by reading a hilarious postcard the late Mr. Hughes sent her during the 1960s.

"Who cares about all these scholars?" Mr. Gordon asks no one in particular. "We're not important. After we're dead, the literature will be the only thing left."

Mr. Gordon liked poet James A. Emanuel, who read *Roller Skate Girl,* a poem about a college professor attracted to one of his students. His wry, sensual words drew laughter from the audience and apparently infuriated two women who nudged and mumbled their way out of a packed amphitheatre.

Relatives of late writers were an even bigger hit. A lively panel featuring Ellen and Julia Wright (widow and daughter of Richard), Lesley Himes (widow of Chester) and 1950s expatriate artists Samuel Allen, Edward Clark, Herbert Gentry and Richard Gibson captivated a standing-room-only crowd of sweating participants.

During a discussion-cum-cocktail party, bad-boy novelist Ishmael Reed "dissed" one French scholar, leaving the intellectual visibly startled after the man questioned the value of black slang in African-American literature. Mr. Reed told his host that black literature was being translated without difficulty in places all over the globe, including Asia. "The Japanese," Mr. Reed added, "pay better than the French."

On the last day of the conference, exhausted participants collapsed behind tables at Haynes Restaurant Americain, a black-American-owned soul food emporium that dishes up black-eyed peas, spicy red beans, smothered cabbage, fried chicken and barbecued ribs. "The fun thing was meeting all the people," Dr. Jackson says. "Not just the folk from other places in the U.S., but from all over the world. We had so many things in common, it was just like a family reunion."

March 15, 1992

What's Shaking

■ ■ ■ ■ ■ ■ ■ ■ ■ ■

Most children's recordings really bug Taj Mahal. A father of seven, the veteran jazz and blues singer/guitarist says he has heard a lot of junk over the years. "That squeaky, squawky 'Hi, Mickey' stuff gets on your nerves," he says. "I know it gets on mine."

To help remedy the situation, Mr. Mahal serves up a funky version of *Hambone*, a clapping rhyme, on *Shake It To The One That You Love The Best: Play Songs and Lullabies from Black Musical Traditions.*

Cheryl Warren-Mattox, the creator of *Shake It*, thought up the project after the birth of her son nearly 10 years ago. A musician, radio programmer and host of radio talk and classical music shows in El Sobrante, Calif., she wanted to share some of the traditional African-American songs she sang as a girl in Oklahoma.

"I was interested in doing children's programs, but couldn't find anything well-produced," Mrs. Mattox says. "I said, 'Why not do it myself?' It took awhile to come to fruition, though."

She arranged the music for *Shake It* in a number of styles to transcend the tinny piano and hollow sounds often found in children's recordings and to expose children to the diversity of black music. She created a classical background for the Creole lullaby *Fais Do Do, Colas.* Other styles include a bouncy reggae rendition of *Jump Shamador,* sassy, swinging jazz versions of *Little Sally Walker* and *Miss Lucy*, and gospel and rhythm-and-blues arrangements of other songs.

Call-and-response, an African tradition that involves one person singing and a group answering, is found in many of the play songs on the first side of *Shake It*. In the collection, adults sing lead and the Shake It Children's Chorus responds.

Vocalists featured on the cassette include Linda Tillery, a member of Grammy Award-winning singer Bobby McFerrin's Voicestra; Kitty Beethoven; Judy Bowen; Najla Id-Deen; Brenda Vaughan; and Joe Mattox, Mrs. Mattox's husband. Taj Mahal, who recorded *Shake Sugary,* his own award-winning children's collection last year, makes a guest appearance on *Hambone.*

The collection reflects a growing trend in children's entertainment, says Jim Deerhawk, vice president of Music For Little People, a Northern California recording and distribution company. Many of today's parents seek toys, books and music that broaden their children's horizons.

Although *Shake It* offers sophisticated arrangements of melodies sung in African-American neighborhoods, the collection is meant for all children. Music For Little People catalog customers, who Mr. Deerhawk says are primarily educated, female, Anglo and "upscale," love the set. The company hasn't compiled statistics, but estimates sales of *Shake It* in the thousands, according to Mr. Deerhawk.

At Black Images Book Bazaar in Dallas, customers bought dozens during the holidays, says co-owner Ashira Tosihwe. "It continues to be a very good item," Ms. Tosihwe adds. "They read the lyrics, and it brings back memories, and they are really fascinated with the artwork."

The collection's packaging contributes to its appeal, says Varnette Honeywood, the Los Angeles-based painter and collage artist whose work appears on the cover. The paperback book rests in the bottom of a square, yellow box; the cassette fits in the upper right-hand corner. A border of Kente cloth, a brightly colored, hand-woven African textile, runs along the left edge of the package. Tiny African symbols — in red and black — accent the box.

"The design is really beautiful," Ms. Honeywood says. "I wish more people would think as creatively as Cheryl (Mattox) does. I am honored to have my work used in this way." One Carrollton mother liked the book cover so much, she framed it and hung it on the wall of her toddler's room.

The 11 full-color illustrations inside showcase the work of Brenda Joysmith and Ms. Honeywood, two well-known African-American painters. "They are two of the best," Mrs. Mattox says. "They already had so many pieces that fit into the family and playtime themes I wanted reflected in *Shake It*."

The 56-page, full-color book provides lyrics and scores for each of the collection's 16 play songs and 10 lullabies. Because of regional variations in lyrics and games, Mrs. Mattox divided them into categories: ring games (played in a circle), line games and clapping rhymes. Although it's not noted in the book, some of the songs offer the syncopated rhythms found in Double Dutch, a fast-paced form of rope jumping.

The American Library Association recognized the collection with a notable award in 1989, and in 1990, the National Association of Independent Record Producers honored it with an Indie Award.

Mrs. Mattox arranged and produced each song, designed the project, selected the art, musicians and singers. "Frankly, Cheryl (Mattox) did all the work," Ms. Honeywood says. "When we're out autographing copies, people tell us they assumed some big company is behind the whole thing."

February 6, 1991

A View
From the Left

■ ■ ■ ■ ■ ■ ■ ■ ■ ■

L OS ANGELES — There's hardly a book about this country's radical political leaders and social movements that doesn't mention Louise Thompson Patterson — labor organizer, human rights activist, friend and assistant to poet Langston Hughes and singer Paul Robeson and mentor to numerous members of America's black artistic and intellectual communities.

Her own book has been 91 years in the making. Finally, she says, she's ready to write it. "I realize that time is of the essence," Mrs. Patterson says. "I hope to get the final draft out this year."

She waited this long out of modesty. Her skills, she says, in no way compare to those of the writers she knew and loved. "I'm not a writer," she says softly. "I was an organizer."

Her organizational coups include pulling together the eclectic band of black artists who traveled to Moscow in 1932 to make a movie about black life in America. In 1949, she booked engagements and arranged security for Mr. Robeson's historic cross-country concert tour.

Writing her memoirs at age 91, she realizes that 'time is of the essence.'

■ ■ ■ ■ ■ ■ ■ ■ ■ ■

She also led the speaking tour featuring mothers of "the Scottsboro boys," a group of young black men who were accused of raping two white women in Scottsboro, Ala. Their 1931 trial became a cause celebre among African Americans, liberal whites and the Communist Party.

Margaret B. Wilkerson, professor and chair of the African American Studies Department at the University of California at Berkeley, regards Mrs. Patterson as a central figure in this century's many human rights movements. "Louise gives us a perspective on our past as a nation," Dr. Wilkerson says. "We're not talking about someone who read about these people. We're not talking about someone who was tangential. We're talking about a woman who worked beside (writer) Zora Neale Hurston, a woman who was key to many activities and movements."

But Mrs. Patterson is distracted this morning and doesn't really want to talk about her past. There are long pauses in the conversation. She explains that she was awake with a sick friend most of the night. She also can't stop thinking about the recent Los Angeles riots, which she calls "rebellion." An Oakland resident, Mrs. Patterson is in Los Angeles, her first visit since the uprising destroyed several of the city's South Central neighborhoods.

Her story, she says, pales when compared with the violence and its horrific implications. "I can't think about the Harlem Renaissance," Mrs. Patterson says. "There is too much unrest, too much frustration here." The destruction, she says, was inevitable. For all the civil rights legislation and economic improvements, the riots — which ignited after four white police officers were acquitted in the videotaped beating of black motorist Rodney King — show how little race relations have evolved.

"I've been thinking about the 1935 uprising in Harlem," she says. "(Fiorello) La Guardia was mayor. The first thing that came to my lips was, 'It's the same old story.' This time, though, they can't blame the communists."

There is some satisfaction in this last remark. During the first half of the century — Mrs. Patterson's heyday, if you will — communists were blamed for most of this country's social woes. In 1940, she married persecuted party leader William Patterson, lawyer for the Scottsboro boys. Her leftist affiliations and open criticism of the U.S. government cost her, says her daughter, MaryLouise Patterson-Gilmer, a Riverside, Calif., pediatrician.

"(Educator) Mary Bethune once called her in and said, 'Child, why you getting mixed up with those Reds?'" Dr. Patterson says. "My mother worked very hard. She chose her life, but it wasn't without its price. My parents didn't have any money. My father went to prison."

Early challenges helped Mrs. Patterson cope with later sacrifices. She grew up the only child of a divorced domestic who worked in tiny towns all over the Pacific Northwest. She was usually the only black child in town. White children ignored her or, worse, made fun of her, says Dr. Patterson, 49, also an only child. "She was the pariah," Dr. Patterson says. "She was the ... child who had no friends."

At Berkeley during the early '20s, Mrs. Patterson experienced further alienation as one of a handful of black students. She graduated with honors in 1923, but the isolation was indelible and further fueled her lifelong obsession with battling racism. "She could have moved into the black middle class," Dr. Patterson says of her mother. "She could have been one of those bridge wives with diamond rings and black maids who live in Washington, D.C." But she chose not to.

Her isolation during college was indelible and further fueled her lifelong obsession with battling racism.

Mrs. Patterson took her idealism to the South, where she taught at the University of Arkansas-Pine Bluff, then at Hampton Institute in Virginia. Discouraged by what she viewed as paternalism by the colleges' then-white administrations, she headed for Harlem — the center of black intellectual life. There, she worked as a secretary to Langston Hughes and Zora Neale Hurston. She taught, organized labor and arts groups and edited a newsletter.

It would be years, though, before she would even consider compiling her own biographical material. Princeton University professor Arnold Rampersad, the award-winning Langston Hughes biographer, says Mrs. Patterson is a talker — conversant on a number of topics, as long as she isn't the subject. She recalls events and players with precision. But her considerable influence is something she keeps private.

"She's a fairly humble person," Dr. Rampersad says. "She's not egotistical at all, but even memoirs require displays of ego." Her lifelong dedication to radical socialism probably influenced her perspective about her own significance, he adds. "She does not want to be introspective," Dr. Rampersad says. "We have to respect that. The party always preached diminution of personality. At the same time, she's extraordinarily charming and extremely intelligent."

Over the years, her daughter says, friends and family have urged Mrs. Patterson to write about her experiences. "It's not like people haven't encouraged her," Dr. Patterson says. "Louise simply isn't one to brag about what she's done, whom she knows or where she's been. Also, there's a privateness about black people of her generation. Then again, she may have been waiting for history to judge her."

Dr. Wilkerson says Mrs. Patterson has opened up a lot during their five-year collaboration. "She understands now how important the personal life is, how the personal relates to political choices," Dr. Wilkerson says. "But Louise is of a generation in which the personal takes a back seat."

Dr. Wilkerson, who is writing a biography about playwright Lorraine Hansberry, met Mrs. Patterson while researching the late author's life. "I didn't know of Louise at all when I started work on Lorraine," she says. "Louise was a mentor to Lorraine, and a deeper knowledge of Louise's life and times has really helped to make my bio of Lorraine a much better book."

Dr. Wilkerson and a changing group of Berkeley students have painstakingly interviewed Mrs. Patterson and recorded her oral history. Transcriptions of these tapes are the basis for the long-awaited memoirs. A Bay Area church, private donors and poet Maya Angelou have raised about $15,000 to pay for clerical help.

"It's marvelous working with someone like Louise," Dr. Wilkerson says. "She's meticulous about collaborative work." And committed to completing the project. Although lung and other health problems have slowed her down this year, she works on the book almost daily.

"People say, 'Louise, when are you going to rest?'" she says. "'When are you going to act your age?' I say, 'When I'm dead.'"

July 8, 1992

SECTION VII

·

THE NEXT GENERATION

···········

In Search of Family

■ ■ ■ ■ ■ ■ ■ ■ ■ ■

The child placement office closed more than an hour ago, but four counselors still frantically work the phones. Devon, just 3 days old, needs some place to sleep. His mother, a woman with no permanent address, slipped out of the hospital without her newborn baby.

Every few minutes, the counselors report why one foster family or another can't take Devon tonight: A child at the Joneses' house has a nasty virus. Mrs. Garcia already has two foster children under 18 months. The Perrys are about to leave for vacation.

Stoically, Diane Wright-Jones, child placement supervisor, reassures the counselors that a foster family will come through. In a few months, someone might even want to adopt Devon.

"Poor baby," says Ms. Jones, stroking the infant's silky black hair. "We had four black boys today. All infants."

It is a tragic and common tale. While white infants and even disabled Romanian babies are snapped up like rare commodities, black children wait.

And wait.

For years, the Texas Department of Human Services has had more black children than available homes. It is a situation mirrored across the United States, where more than 18,000 black children — half the nation's adoptable children — wait for families, according to the Philadel-

While white infants and even disabled Romanian babies are snapped up like rare commodities, black children wait.

■ ■ ■ ■ ■ ■ ■ ■ ■ ■

163

phia-based National Adoption Center. The non-profit agency, which serves as a clearinghouse for adoption information and referrals, reports that this figure represents a 17 percent increase over five years ago.

Devon's birth on Christmas Day increased the swelling pool of adoptable black children who live in foster homes and institutions in the Dallas-Fort Worth area.

He is one of more than 250 adoptable black children the state agency attempted to place in 1991. By comparison, the department had custody of more than 269 adoptable white children and more than 223 Hispanic children. But because blacks make up about 12 percent of the U.S. and Texas populations (Hispanics make up about 25.5 percent of the state population), the figure for adoptable black children is disproportionately high. Black children also wait for adoptive families an average of nearly eight months longer than their white counterparts. Here and across the country, the flow of abandoned, abused and neglected black children outpaces the capacity of caseworkers to place them.

Most black children become adoptable when the state terminates parental rights.

■ ■ ■ ■ ■ ■ ■ ■ ■ ■

"Last year we had about 70 adoptable black children," Ms. Wright-Jones says. "This year Dallas County and Tarrant County (where Fort Worth is located) had 104 at the beginning of December."

In some instances, a black woman decides while she is pregnant to give up her child, says Nyla Stewart, director of special services for Hope Cottage, a private adoption agency. When she makes this decision, the woman usually is referred to a private or church-affiliated adoption agency. At these agencies, adoptive parents pay fees up to $20,000 to cover the birth mother's medical care, lawyers' bills and other costs associated with childbirth and adoption.

But most black children become adoptable when the state terminates parental rights, Ms. Wright-Jones says. Rights are removed as a last resort — after all efforts to rehabilitate a family are unsuccessful. Most parents who lose permanent custody have a history of abuse or neglect.

"The goal is to keep families together," Ms. Wright-Jones says. "We try to get parents into counseling, drug-treatment programs, parenting classes — whatever it takes. But unemployment and the drug epidemic have hit us rather hard."

Prospective parents find children with those backgrounds undesirable, says Sidney Beal Jr., assistant pastor of Concord Missionary Baptist Church. A father of four who adopted two preschoolers last spring, the minister says he and his wife didn't consider adopting an older child.

"Our son was taken from his parents at 7 months," Mr. Beal says. "He had fractured ribs. When he first came here, he had nightmares. He would hide. One time we found him under the bed. He's calm now. I think he would have had more trouble trusting us had he been older. We didn't want a child 8, 9, 10 years old. We didn't want to chance disciplinary problems."

Hoping that someone might take those risks, a local volunteer organization — the 6-year-old Minority Adoption Council — has forged an alliance with public and private adoption agencies and area businesses.

"Anyone who has a child is taking a risk," says Rose Pounders, a founder of the council. "Who knows how a child would be with love and guidance? A lot of these children are afraid of adults. They have their own set of values, true. But being a parent to any child takes time, takes patience. Parents never know how a birth child will come out."

The council, a group of Dallas and Fort Worth black adoptive parents and other advocates, sets up information booths at community fairs, speaks at black churches, acts as a liaison between prospective parents and the state Department of Human Services and organizes events to showcase available black children.

Days before Christmas, the council hosted a Christmas party that attracted 2,000 people. The event, sponsored by a local radio station that targets black listeners, featured all 104 adoptable black children in the Dallas-Fort Worth area. As prospective parents looked on, the youngest children stuffed themselves with chocolate-iced cake and donated McDonald's burgers. The older ones looked bored or tense. As they paraded across the stage one by one to whisper to Santa (Dallas Cowboys lineman Nate Newton), disc jockey Tom Joyner delivered brief biographical sketches.

Percy and Barbara Edwards watched the children intently. The couple, who live in a Dallas suburb, want a healthy male infant, and they cuddled up to 8-month-old David, a chubby-cheeked baby with thick, curly hair. As they held him, a volunteer snapped a portrait of the potential family. The couple — both work for IBM, he as an auditor, she as an analyst — then left the ballroom to quietly flip through binders of photos and biographies of available children. In David's biography, they learned that the boy's mother is HIV positive. Although the baby hasn't tested positive for the virus that causes AIDS, his prognosis remains uncertain.

"I don't know much about AIDS," Mrs. Edwards says later. "The uncertainty is not something I'm willing to handle."

The Edwardses like David so much, though, that they crossed their fingers and registered for 10 weeks of parenting classes required by the Department of Human Services. If David tests positive at any time during the adoption process, the Edwardses will wait for a healthy baby.

Mrs. Pounders, a mother of three, two of whom are adopted, is heartened by the Edwardses' interest. In all, the Minority Adoption Council party resulted in 65 inquiries from prospective parents. "That is very good," Mrs. Pounders says. "My first caseworker commented to me that black people don't adopt. I told her, 'That's not true. There's just a lack of awareness in our community.'" All we know about is private agencies. A lot of our people can't afford to pay fees charged by the private homes, not even the ones that offer a sliding (fee) scale for minority parents."

Increased information is bound to stimulate interest among blacks, Mrs. Pounders believes. She says blacks crave family life as much as other Americans do.

"We have stable families just like every other race," Mrs. Pounders says. "We work for the same lifestyles that everyone does." And black and white infertility rates are nearly equal, says William Mosher, a statistician with the National Center for Health Statistics.

"The figures may not be consistent with the perception of some, including physicians, but that is simply because those with more income and insurance coverage are more likely to seek infertility treatment or pursue adoption."

Buoyed by such facts, the Minority Adoption Council is determined to match children and families — hopefully black families. The council, the Department of Human Services and the National Association of Black Social Workers advocate same-race placements.

"Being adopted is a big enough issue for a child to deal with," says Carol Brandon, spokeswoman for the council. "When a child is placed transracially, that creates confusion about culture, race, those sorts of issues. Problems can be as basic as a white parent not knowing how to maintain a black child's hair. Immersion in his or her own culture helps the child develop an identity. It helps him feel good about himself."

But because transracial adoptions are the only option for some black children, the council and the state do not actively oppose the practice. They hope to limit it, however, through efforts such as the One Church One Child program, through which black ministers actively seek and support adoptive parents among their congregations. The group lobbies the Department of Human Services to get as many blacks as possible on television news segments that feature children who need adopting.

The couple's 9-year-old son had his class praying that he would get a baby brother.

■ ■ ■ ■ ■ ■ ■ ■ ■ ■

Mr. Beal, 48, and his wife, Carolyn, 38, praise such televised efforts. Without them, they might not have added 2-year-old Briana and her 3-year-old brother, Joseph, to their family. Without them, the cherubic toddlers might have languished in foster care until they reached 18. The Beals, who live in the Dallas suburb of DeSoto, consider the council's work a religious and political mission.

"It's an African-American community thing," Mr. Beal says. "We need to take a more active role in adopting children who some of our people cannot care for."

The couple's 9-year-old son, Brandon, had his class praying that he would get a baby brother, Mrs. Beal says. Last spring, he got a brother and sister.

"We know God willed for us to have these children," says Mrs. Beal, rocking Briana in her lap. "They've brought us nothing but joy."

January 4, 1992

Comic Relief

■■■■■■■■■■

He doesn't fly, scale buildings, possess fantastic powers or wear a slick costume. But Brotherman has one trait most comic-book heroes don't: He is an African-American — one of the first to have an entire comic book devoted to his adventures. He is assistant district attorney by day, vigilante by night.

Sound familiar?

It should and it shouldn't, says David Sims, who created the book with his brothers Guy and Jason. David draws the characters, Guy writes the text, and Jason runs the production and marketing end of Big City Comics, the Dallas-based family firm that publishes Brotherman.

'We look at Brotherman as being the black hero of the 1990s.'

■■■■■■■■■■

"The story line is typical — the vigilante in the big city — but it's from our perspective," says David, who is 25. "We look at Brotherman as being the black hero of the 1990s."

In order to capture the imaginations of African-American readers, the Simses have created a fantasy world that is unmistakably ethnic. David's drawings show a range of skin tones, hair textures and facial and body features. In describing one female character, two catty bank tellers say, "She ain't all that fresh." Fresh is a hip-hop synonym for sexy.

Characters include African-American professionals, as well as individuals from more humble backgrounds. The first issue focuses on Brotherman's bumbling pursuit of a woman.

The Simses' father, Edward Sims Jr., director of the Center for

Multicultural Research and Training at a Dallas-area community college, exposed his sons to all kinds of art and literature, including comic books. With their mother, Dallas educator Deanna Sims, the couple founded Black Family Rituals, a company that has published multicultural educational texts for more than two decades. The idea for Brotherman grew out of that exposure.

"I got into comics in third grade," David says. "I started noticing there weren't a lot of black characters in the books. In eighth grade, I burned all my collection. I didn't feel like they reflected us."

His disaffection is typical of African Americans, who have only a tenuous relationship with the comic-book industry. Marketing surveys have not sought to define the industry's minority audience nationally, but only about 10 percent of the patrons who frequent Lone Star Comics & Science Fiction, a popular Dallas-area store, are African American, says its manager, Alan Durham.

'I started noticing there weren't a lot of black characters in the (comic) books.'

■ ■ ■ ■ ■ ■ ■ ■ ■ ■

Minorities make up just 10 to 15 percent of the fans who attend the largest national comic conventions, says Maggie Thompson, co-editor of *Comics Buyer's Guide*, a newspaper for comics collectors.

A number of factors help explain African Americans' lack of enthusiasm for comic books. For starters, the industry concentrates its advertising campaigns in stores specializing in comic-book sales. Beyond that, Ms. Thompson says, education and economics come into play.

"There is a higher illiteracy rate among our minority populations," Ms. Thompson says. "Also, disposable income, with which people purchase reading materials as entertainment, could be a limiting factor."

The brothers hope to overcome the status quo by placing Brotherman not only in comic-book stores but in shops that cater to African Americans. For instance, Black Images Book Bazaar, a Dallas emporium that sells titles by and about African Americans, carries the comic.

"Customers are buying it for nostalgic reasons," says Emma Rodgers, co-owner of Black Images. "They are also saying they are glad to see a comic book from the African-American perspective."

Right now, the brothers are pushing their publication at conventions on the East Coast, says Jason Sims, the 26-year-old production manager. The trio couldn't stock enough copies when they introduced the book at the New York Black Expo, a recent trade show for African-American businesses that attracted more than 50,000. So far, the Simses have sold about half of the 10,000 first-run copies printed at a cost of about $5,000.

Ms. Thompson says the Simses' direct-marketing approach is one that has proven successful for other independent comic-book producers. "It allows a small publication like Big City Comics to print a small run, pay their expenses and maybe make a small profit," she says. The Simses' book arrives at a time when comic books are enjoying tremendous growth, says Ms. Thompson. New readers are discovering comics, and old ones are returning to the fold after seeing adaptations such as Teenage Mutant Ninja Turtles, Batman and others on the silver screen. These successes inspire David Sims.

"If you look at the Ninja Turtles," he says, "the creators were just two guys ...."

Brotherman is not the only comic book with African-American characters, but it is the only one whose sole purpose is the portrayal of an African-American title character. It is also the only one created by an African-American company. Although Hispanic, Native American and African-American characters have been around for several decades, minority characters have traditionally appeared as part of crime-fighting groups, Ms. Thompson says.

Marcus McLaurin, the only black editor at Marvel Comics, says a trend is emerging.

"We have more stories in which characters explore the ways they are different from others," he says. "Today, we're getting away from typical racial stereotypes. Minority characters are written as characters. In the '70s, there were more stereotypes like on television. Black characters wore gaudy costumes that were not like super heroes' costumes."

The industry is sensitive about portraying positive racial characteristics, says Buddy Saunders, owner of Lone Star Comics & Science Fiction. The majority of writers and artists, who are white, fear the wrath of the reading audience. In late 1989, for example, an uproar forced Aircel Comics to cancel RIPPER. Readers complained that the first issue depicted African-American characters as large-lipped, dialect-spewing, alcohol-guzzling idiots.

The industry has done the easy thing when dealing with racial issues, Mr. Saunders says. Failures generally have been in the omission of black characters, not in degrading portrayals.

In addition to other independently produced comics, Brotherman will face competition from books published by Marvel Comics and DC, the Ford and General Motors of comics. Together, the two companies control 75 percent of the market.

Mr. McLaurin at Marvel says his company has a minor stable of black characters and seven strong black characters among the 60 titles published each month. This summer the comic-book giant will release *Tales from the Heart of Africa*, a 47-page, full-color book that examines conflicts between people of different cultures.

David Sims, like Brotherman, is undaunted by the challenges. "If I sit back and say, 'We shouldn't press on because others tried it and it didn't work' or 'We're too small to hang in there,' we might as well not try."

May 29, 1990

When Children Become Violent

■ ■ ■ ■ ■ ■ ■ ■ ■ ■

Craig S., 16, multiple assaults; alcoholic stepfather, mother unemployed.

Jerry R., 17, murder; father unknown and mother incarcerated. Mike C., 14, drug dealing and possession of weapon; no contact with father since he was a toddler, mother addicted to drugs. Hugh M., 15, burglary and drug trafficking; one hand disfigured — from being submerged in boiling water by his mother, a crack addict. His father is also a drug addict ...

The roll call at Dallas House.

Just a partial reading of the residents' list reveals conditions few people, including the boys who live in the halfway house operated by the Texas Youth Commission, want to acknowledge. Behind nearly every name is a story of violent crime, lost childhoods and varying degrees of parental neglect.

Robert Louis, treatment coordinator at the house, is emotionless as he reads aloud the list of residents and their crimes. His voice is matter-of-fact.

It is the voice of a man who, after working for 20 years with 10- to 17-year-old boys who commit serious crimes and their families — has ceased to be surprised by what he encounters daily.

'I've gone to more funerals and murder trials in the last three years than in the previous 17 combined.'

■ ■ ■ ■ ■ ■ ■ ■ ■ ■

The toll this has taken on the lives of young African Americans, Mr. Louis says, is mind-boggling.

"I've gone to more funerals and murder trials in the last three years than in the previous 17 combined," he says. "Some days I have to rush from a trial to attend a funeral."

Many of the offenses involve murder and assault with weapons. It's hard for a visitor to believe such rage could lurk behind such sincere and earnest-looking faces.

But Robert Louis knows better. He sees lots of faces.

■ Nearly half of the 24 youths who live at Dallas House are African Americans.

■ In 1992, more than half of the 595 youths committed to Texas Youth Commission facilities for violent offenses — robbery, rape, homicide and other crimes against people — were African Americans. Hispanic and white youths, by comparison, each accounted for 22 percent of the incarcerations for violent crimes.

■ In 1987, African Americans constituted 27 percent of those committed to the Texas Youth Commission, compared to 44 percent in 1992. The share of Hispanic youths committed to the state-run agency declined from 41 percent to 37 percent during that period, whites from 31 percent to 18 percent.

In the wake of the race-related violence after the Dallas Cowboys' recent Super Bowl victory parade and the almost daily accounts of assaults and murders among young African-American people, public officials, ministers, educators and others are asking: Who has the answer for these numbers?

African-American youths are no more troubled than their white peers, maintains James H. Cone, professor of theology at Union Theological Seminary in New York City.

Black youths and their parents, he says, lack the same resources as whites to keep them out of the criminal justice system. The system, therefore, is cast in a parental role far more often for African-American youths, he adds.

Dr. Cone and other specialists who study family issues say that many white adolescents feel a sense of alienation similar to that experienced by their black peers. But they are quick to add that black and white youths play out their frustration in different ways. "Black kids commit genocide," Dr. Cone says, referring to black-on-black crime that often has been described as misplaced anger at whites for the conditions that exist in the African-American community.

"White kids kill themselves. The rate of suicide is much higher among white kids than black kids," he says.

White youths, especially those in the middle and upper classes, have parents who can afford private rehabilitation programs, Mr. Louis adds. At the first sign of legal trouble and behavioral problems, many white parents institutionalize their children, he adds.

"Go on out to these private psychiatric hospitals," he says."They're filled with white teenagers. Black families don't have the option to take care of these problems outside of the system."

Mr. Louis says many of the white teenagers sent to Dallas House have already received thousands of dollars in private care. "How many black parents have those kinds of benefits?" he asks. "One white family spent $200,000 to keep their kid out of the penal system, and he ended up here anyway."

Many researchers connect the rise in violence among black youths to the disintegration of the African-American family.

Until the 1970s, most black families were intact, says Amos Wilson, a psychology professor at the Bronx, N.Y., campus of the College of New Rochelle. "There is a direct relationship between unemployment and the breakup of the black family. There is a direct relationship between the breakup of the black family and the levels of violence we are seeing among black children," he says.

The unemployment rate among black males in this country was 13 percent in January, compared with 7.1 percent for the overall population, U.S. Labor Department statistics show.

> 'There is a direct relationship between the breakup of the black family and the levels of violence ... among black children.'
>
> ■ ■ ■ ■ ■ ■ ■ ■ ■ ■ ■

With unemployment has come a steady rise in homes headed by single females and African-American males who are prevented from contributing to the care of their families or from being seen as marriage prospects. Given these conditions, to point the finger at African-American parents — especially single mothers — is to blame the victims, says Barbara Sugland, a researcher with Child Trends, a nonprofit Washington think tank that analyzes children's issues.

Many black single mothers are preoccupied with survival — buying clothing and food, paying rent and finding health care. Supervising their children and participating in family-oriented activities often gets shunted aside, Dr. Sugland says.

"How can a mother think: 'The PTA is next week,' or, 'I need to see Mrs. Smith, the math teacher,' when she is worried about a leaky house with no heat?" she asks.

"Laying responsibility on the parent without laying it on within the context of the whole society is unfair."

The problems of society certainly contribute to the actions of young African Americans and other juveniles, but families — parents especially — should shoulder a share of the responsibility for the behavior of their children, says State District Judge Hal Gaither, who hears juvenile cases.

Many black single parents are preoccupied with survival — not the next PTA meeting.

■ ■ ■ ■ ■ ■ ■ ■ ■ ■

"Parents do not supervise their children properly," Mr. Gaither says. "If parents were doing their job, we wouldn't have as many of the juvenile crime problems we have."

Mr. Gaither says judges in the juvenile system are frustrated. And what angers him most, he says, is parents who ignore court orders. That leaves him, he says, to wonder how such parents can possibly impart a sense of responsibility to their own children.

How can African-American parents be held responsible, some experts ask, when they fall prey to the same problems that plague their children? Listen to these comments from a Dallas Independent School District sixth-grade teacher, who wants to be anonymous because he fears reprisals for his candor. He speaks of pupils who live with drug-addicted parents and guardians:

"Many could not be called parents except in the sense they have a biological connection to these children. Most of my children are responsible for feeding themselves and getting themselves to school in the morning."

The teacher, an African-American man, says his students rarely have school supplies and often are not adequately dressed.

Consequently, he says, he spends more time disciplining his distracted students than instructing them. He has visited students' homes to plead for cooperation from parents. Several parents have admitted that they cannot control their children.

"There seems to be very little in terms of guidance, instruction or explanation of the world," the teacher says. Add criminality and disease, and you have a very self-defeating situation, he says. Steven Kossman, director of juvenile services for the Dallas County Juvenile Department, says many parents who lack parenting skills give birth when they are still children.

"One of the fastest-growing phenomena in our culture is 14-year-olds who give birth," Mr. Kossman says. "A 15-year-old with two kids is not unusual in our system."

The lives of these young parents are more confused today than they were in the past, says Margaret Beale Spencer, a developmental psychology professor and an expert on black child development at Emory University in Atlanta.

Young parents have fewer advocates and fewer examples to follow because the older black middle class has fled the inner cities, she says. "There are class and caste issues that are expressed ... that have not been addressed within the African-American community," Dr. Spencer says. "The mobility of the black middle class doesn't excuse its responsibility to all black children. What I am advocating is a sense of interdependence."

Because African Americans have become more mobile since integration, young parents lack the support and guidance they once received from their extended families, says Dr. Wilson. He has studied black adolescent male violence and its impact on the black family. "A child's reputation and the family reputation is not as precious as it used to be," Dr. Wilson says. "The behavior of children is no longer the stimulus for family shame. Black families once had social standing in a community of people. Now most families in the inner city are homogenous."

Elected officials who slash social programs that support these families while emphasizing the return to so-called family values are failing to acknowledge the underlying causes of inner-city violence, Dr. Wilson says.

"It's but another American myth to think teaching values will solve these problems," he says. "It's a myth to think that love between a black man and black woman will solve these problems. A child cannot eat values."

February 28, 1993

Rite of Passage

■ ■ ■ ■ ■ ■ ■ ■ ■ ■

K amili Johnson speaks of confidence. Though she's just 16, her words do not express the cocksure confidence of youth. As African drums softly beat in the background, the Dallas high school student talks about the difficult transition she's making from childhood to womanhood.

As Kamili speaks, her mother looks at her with an expression that combines relief and pride. A congregation of churchgoers interjects encouraging words.

"No matter what happened," Miss Johnson says, "black women have picked themselves up and started something new or gone on."

Kamili Johnson is participating in an African-rooted rite-of-passage ceremony — a ritual to mark the transition from childhood to adult life. She and three other Dallas-area girls have just completed 13 weeks of initiation classes during which they learned about adult responsibilities. The ancient rite-of-passage program was re-created by a group of African-American mothers who want to provide their daughters with a cultural and historical foundation to face modern America.

Like most parents, mothers of the initiates read the papers and watch the news. Events seem to suggest that no matter how hard the mothers try, some evil force — drugs, premarital sex, bad grades, anything unexpected — could ruin their children's lives. Sandra Washington, one of the mothers, says she reached a frightening conclusion about their kids.

"They did not seem responsible," Mrs. Washington says. "They just wanted to go to school, go to parties, go to school. They were not aware of their responsibilities to the community, to the church." When the mothers read a magazine article about a formal initiation into adulthood, they knew the African-rooted process would provide the girls with the resources they need to steel themselves against a troubled world.

African rites of passage are centuries old. They gradually appeared on the East and West coasts of the United States during the late 1970s and have been spreading slowly across the country.

"It's just now catching on in Dallas," says Ashira Tosihwe. Co-owner of Black Images Book Bazaar, Ms. Tosihwe was hired by Dallas parents to design a three-month program for 11 girls. Also a licensed social worker, she specializes in her practice in youth and family development.

Although the group met at St. Luke's Community United Methodist Church in Southeast Dallas, a predominantly black inner-city neighborhood, the girls live in predominantly white Dallas suburbs.

They learned about spirituality, sexuality, friendship and family.

■ ■ ■ ■ ■ ■ ■ ■ ■ ■

"It's somewhat easy living out here to lose a sense of self," says Toni Johnson, whose daughters attend schools in the North Dallas suburb of Richardson. "One of the reasons we attend St. Luke's is so the girls will have a balance in their lives. They need to know who they are, who their people are. Our children need to know their connection to the African-American community and to Africa."

The St. Luke's group attended two-hour classes at the church each Sunday. The girls listened to lectures and watched films. They conducted research and played games related to African and African-American history and culture. They learned about spirituality, sexuality, career development, financial management, social values, friendship and family, responsibility and self-esteem.

The girls say they initially were reluctant to embrace the rites program because it interfered with their social plans and set them apart from most of their peers.

"It was giving up a lot of weekends," says Mrs. Washington's daughter Dorishane, 18, of the North Dallas suburb of Plano. "At first I didn't like it, but I went in with an open mind. It turned out pretty interesting." In fact, seven of the original 11 girls did not last through the academically and physically rigorous process.

"We lost several girls because of time constraints," Dorishane's mother says. "Others were more interested in being debutantes. We wanted our girls to have something with more meaning."

Watching documentaries on the problems and solutions of domestic workers in New Orleans and South Africa, says Miss Washington, motivated her to accept challenges. She used to expect her parents to pay for everything. Now she puts her earnings from an after-school job toward car maintenance and college savings.

"It showed me I can get anything done," Miss Washington says. "It made me aware of obstacles that might occur and made me think of how I'll be better prepared to handle them."

Ms. Tosihwe stimulated the girls' interest by relating their studies to their own experiences. Homework assignments included interviewing family members and researching family Bibles and scrapbooks. The information was used to compile detailed genealogies, to provide materials for an ancestral display that was a focal point of the ceremony and to discover something they didn't already know about their families.

"The goal was to give them a subjective feeling for history," Ms. Tosihwe says. "If they understand their personal history, then they can expand the circle to their community and to a larger context. One of the girls became excited when she found that cousins in her generation have personalities and traits similar to her great-great aunts'."

In a session devoted to sexuality, the girls learned that premarital sex for women is frowned upon in many traditional African cultures. To understand the consequences of their own sexual choices, the girls played a board game. Impulsive answers led them on paths that included unwanted pregnancy and sexually transmitted diseases. Deliberate choices led them to careers and stable family life.

The tone of a few of the classes made the girls feel as if they were being beaten over the head with warnings they had learned to heed long ago.

"It was a lot of fun," says Robin Marshall, 16, a student at a Dallas high school. "But everybody wants to tell us about sex. We hear it at school. We hear it at church. We hear it from our parents. We hear it every day."

The initiation process lasts from several weeks to a year, depending on the number of objectives set by individual groups. Beginning in August, the St. Luke's group met for three months. Part of the process involved a survival-skills retreat similar to what initiates undergo in Africa. The girls, their mothers and Ms. Tosihwe used ropes and wits to overcome a range of physical challenges. They scaled eight-foot walls, walked across suspended logs and performed other feats during the course.

In Africa, advisers take adolescent boys and girls into the forest to teach them tribal and family history and hunting and cultivation techniques. Separating teens from the tribe emphasizes their need to depend on one another to survive.

Because overcoming each obstacle required cooperation, Robin Marshall says, the course tested the girls' trust for one another and revealed their capacity for teamwork.

"We had to use sign language to communicate," Miss Marshall says. "When we were on the rope, it took inner strength to make our physical strength work." Mothers were invited to join the girls for some sessions. For others, the girls met with Ms. Tosihwe alone. When the girls and women separated, the mothers participated in independent discussion and lecture groups. Both groups attended a wrap-up discussion at the end of each Sunday class.

Dallas psychologist Brenda Wall, an African American, praises her community's rites of passage as necessary for child-rearing.

"It's insightful for adults to recognize the need for a very deliberate process that reinforces identity," Dr. Wall says. "Children need values that are transmitted for generations. It's good for children to deal with structure, expectation and authority."

Rites of passage work by forcing black adolescents and their families to acknowledge and celebrate the subtle, significant characteristics that distinguish them from their white peers, Dr. Wall says. Those differences include fewer opportunities, less reinforcement and encouragement from the entire community and fewer resources, she says.

"If you deny the fact that you're different, pretend like everyone is the same or act like there are no special problems, then you won't be equipped to handle them when they arise."

Agencies in at least seven other American cities assist community groups or families in African rites-of-passage programs.

Although girls or boys generally participate in single-sex groups, coed classes are sometimes formed. The first initiates in Dallas were boys and girls who participated in rites of passage as part of a late 1970s summer jobs program at the Bethlehem Foundation, a social service agency.

Rites of passage are as individual as the communities that hold them. The St. Luke's ceremony was held on the final day of Kwanzaa, a weeklong holiday that glorifies black culture and its African roots. About 150 observers sat on the edge of the pews in the dimly lit chapel. They listened to colorfully cloaked African drummers who set a rhythm for the two-hour evening program. Dressed in black shifts and tunics of patterned African fabrics, the mothers of the four girls danced first while Ms. Tosihwe stood chanting at the altar. After the mothers took their places, the girls danced down the church aisles. Like their peers in Africa, the girls punctuated their promenade with solo performances of their own choreography.

Like their African peers, the girls punctuated their promenade with solo performances.

Female community leaders — an educator, a politician, a businesswoman, a minister, a judge and Ms. Tosihwe — then greeted the girls and encouraged them to vigorously pursue their goals, lift their community and respect their God and family. To symbolize the passage to womanhood, mothers followed the African tradition of wrapping the girls' heads in cloth. Toward the program's end, fathers performed their only rite-of-passage role by offering gifts to their daughters. (Fathers participate more actively in rites for boys.)

After the ceremony, observers and participants attended a reception in a large meeting room that featured an ornate ancestral display. Birth certificates, childhood photos, scrapbooks, large fertility dolls and other mementos from each girl's family adorned a round table covered in African prints and laden with an African ceramic vessel filled with bird-of-paradise and eucalyptus leaves.

Alice Shaw-Sims, 26, attributes many of her successes to a late 1970s rite of passage led by Ms. Tosihwe at the Bethlehem Foundation. Ms. Shaw-Sims returned to the agency, where she is now a social work aide.

"I was going through a lot of things, and it helped me deal with my family situation instead of running away," Ms. Shaw-Sims says. "I stayed in school. I graduated. The program made me more sensitive toward others."

'Now I can speak up without feeling that people are looking down on me.'

■ ■ ■ ■ ■ ■ ■ ■ ■ ■

Lessons learned during rites classes are designed to help initiates adapt to an often-hostile environment. All of the girls in the St. Luke's group intimately know the sense of alienation that develops from being one of a few black students attending a predominantly white school.

Gabraelle Lane, 16, says that before she participated in the rites classes she would bristle and remain silent whenever one of her schoolmates said something derogatory about blacks and other minorities. She was often reluctant to speak out because she feared appearing preachy or different from other students.

"I would get offended, but I didn't want to say anything," Miss Lane says. "Now I can speak up without feeling that people are looking down on me."

"The main thing I got out of this was to have confidence in myself," says Kamili Johnson, "because no matter what I might do, if I try, there is no way that I can fail."

January 21, 1990

SECTION VIII

·

A WOMAN'S BURDEN

··········

Women of Decision

■ ■ ■ ■ ■ ■ ■ ■ ■ ■

icole Martin wears her curly black hair in a ponytail on top of her head. The summer sun has brought out a band of brown freckles across the bridge of her nose. She's 20, but looks younger. She's also black, single and pregnant.

At first, Ms. Martin says, she planned to have an abortion.

"We'd gotten the money together," she says. "Then my boyfriend changed his mind."

The decision to carry her pregnancy to term was difficult and confusing. She felt pressured to have the baby by her high school sweetheart, whom she no longer sees, but her mother tried to convince her that parenthood is difficult under the best of circumstances. She's a college student and says her mother feared that she wouldn't earn her degree. Several weeks into the pregnancy, Ms. Martin says, she still isn't sure if she made the right decision.

"I've been scared to talk to people," she says. "Sometimes now I wish I had gone on and had an abortion."

'Sometimes now I wish I had gone on and had an abortion.'

■ ■ ■ ■ ■ ■ ■ ■ ■ ■

Although Ms. Martin never has marched or donated a dime to an abortion rights group, she says she's glad for the opportunity to make a choice. In fact, she adds, she considers abortion protests a "white" activity she can't begin to comprehend.

Like many black women, she doesn't see abortion as a political issue. And although black women have abortions at a proportionally higher rate than their white peers, they generally perceive the issue in personal and financial terms.

"I can't understand why white people are so much against abortion," Ms. Martin says. "They protest so much. You can hardly turn on the television or pick up a paper without them screaming about abortion.... They should just face the fact that people are going to have abortions anyway, even if they can't get one from a doctor."

Her views parallel those of most black women, according to a one study. The 1991-1992 Women of Color Reproductive Health Poll found that 83 percent of black women favor a woman's right to make her own decision about abortion. The study, co-sponsored by the Communications Consortium Media Center and the National Council of Negro Women, also found that 85 percent of black women said it is wrong for abortion rights opponents to block entrances to abortion clinics.

Poll results disprove the notion that black women have little or no interest in the abortion debate.

■ ■ ■ ■ ■ ■ ■ ■ ■ ■

But that doesn't mean there is unity on the abortion issue. Michele Jackson, spokeswoman for the 7-year-old Washington, D.C.-based Black Americans for Life, dismisses the study's findings.

"Black people, by and large, are against abortion as an alternative to a crisis pregnancy situation," Ms. Jackson says. "Studies show that. I don't know the percentages, but I do know that when black women are offered the chance to carry their babies to term, they opt for that."

The study's results come from two nationwide surveys of 1,157 African-American, Hispanic, Asian and Native American women conducted between May 1991 and March 1992. It was conducted by the Winters Group Inc., an independent Rochester, N.Y., polling firm, for the council, a 57-year-old civil rights group, and the consortium, a nonprofit, nonpartisan group that provides media consultations for other nonprofit organizations.

Poll results disprove the notion that black women have little or no interest in the abortion debate, says Emily Tynes, deputy director of the Washington, D.C.-based Communications Consortium.

It is a belief stemming from the fact that blacks, with a few exceptions, have been virtually invisible and voiceless in the politics of abortion.

"If you measure black women's participation by the faces you see at marches and protests, then you miss the story," Ms. Tynes says. "For many of them, marching is a luxury. Black women have not organized around this issue, and part of the problem has been the messenger. If we see white, middle-class women in the news, then we think that surely, this is not our issue."

That perception and the reality are slowly changing.

In the last two years, battle by battle, black women and organizations that represent them have increasingly lent their support to the abortion rights movement. The National Council of Negro Women is lobbying Chicago-area voters to use an upcoming referendum to restore publicly funded abortions to Cook County Hospital. The National Coalition of 100 Black Women has initiated an abortion rights education program.

Akua Furlow, spokeswoman for the 2,000-member Texas Black Americans for Life, equates the increase in abortion rights activities among blacks with genocide.

"Black women do not realize that the people forcing abortion on our people as a panacea to our social problems have a long history of beliefs in eugenics," says Mr. Furlow, a former social worker. "They have a long history of racism."

But findings of the Women of Color poll contradict her assertion. The study found that 76 percent of black women reject the idea that birth control and abortion are tools intended to help eliminate the black race.

Sixteen prominent black women, including former U.S. Rep. Shirley Chisholm, U.S. Rep. Maxine Waters (D-California) and Rep. Cardiss Collins (D-Illinois), economist and columnist Julianne Malveaux and *Ms. Magazine* editor Marcia Ann Gillespie, have formed an independent, ad hoc committee to wage a national campaign against abortion restrictions.

Dr. Dorothy Height, 80, president of the National Council of Negro Women, says committee members organized to combat the perception that abortion rights is not a priority among black women. In an attempt to overcome black religious and social customs that render abortion a taboo topic among many blacks, the committee distributed a strongly worded brochure. Planned Parenthood Federation of America is also a sponsor of the brochure.

"One of the great myths of America is the purported moral looseness of black women," Dr. Height says. "That myth has embarrassed black women and affected the extent to which we freely discuss and come forward on issues relating to sexuality, including abortion."

The committee's statement, which draws its style and essence from the breadth of black oratory, makes an analogy between abortion rights and blacks' struggle for civil and human rights. In dramatic language, the essay discusses how black women were used as breeders during slavery.

'One of the great myths of America is the purported moral looseness of black women.'

■ ■ ■ ■ ■ ■ ■ ■ ■ ■

"Choice is the essence of freedom," the essay says. "It's what we African Americans have struggled for all these years. The right to choose where we would sit on a bus. The right to vote.... Those of us who remember the bad old days when Jim Crow ruled and segregation was the way of things, know the hardships and indignities we faced. Somebody said where we could live, where we could work, what schools we could go to.... Somebody's saying that we must have babies whether we choose to or not.... Meanwhile, those somebodies who claim they're pro-life aren't moved to help the living."

Black women's groups, traditionally focused on survival issues such as employment, education, nutrition, crime and housing, are embracing abortion rights out of frustration, Dr. Height says. Larger, predominantly white groups that support or oppose abortion rights generally have overlooked the priorities of blacks and other ethnic minorities — though nonwhites annually receive half the abortions performed in the United States.

"Our difference from majority groups is that we have not made this a single issue the way they have," Dr. Height says. "We do not view abortion as an issue apart from the many elements of family planning: maternal health, prenatal care, infant mortality and the whole dismal health situation facing minority women and children with limited access to health care services."

Thelma Wallace, a black registered nurse, says she chose an abortion 17 years ago for personal rather than political reasons. The Dallas widow, who volunteers with several community groups, recently decided to speak out in favor of abortion rights because she believes opponents have little respect for women's vastly different individual circumstances.

"I always say I'm pro-choice," she says. "A lot of times, black people don't want to hear it. In the black community, you don't hear us talking about sex, but obviously, a lot of us partake.

"I have five children who I love dearly," Ms. Wallace adds. "I believe in family. Being a mother is the most rewarding role in my life. But no one can tell me, or any other woman, what we can or cannot handle. These protesters, who don't know me or the women they harass outside of abortion clinics, can't keep me or anyone else from making a decision about something that ultimately is my responsibility.

"These people, who don't seem to be concerned about all the black children in foster care that no one (cares) about, have chosen an issue that is safe to choose," Ms. Wallace says. "It's easy to jump on women. It's easier to jump on black women, because so many of us are alone, so many of us are single."

Black organizations that support abortion rights are attempting to harness the energy of people such as Thelma Wallace. The time has come to politicize the issue because black women stand to lose a great deal if abortion is restricted further, says Robert Prince of Dallas, a black doctor who serves as a National Abortion Rights Action League board member.

"Three out of four women who inquire about abortion at my South Dallas office end up having the baby," Dr. Prince says. "For a lot of black women, $250 is a lot of money to amass on short notice. The decision by the federal government to withdraw abortion funding for low-income women condemned many black women to compulsory pregnancy."

Adoption is not an attractive option because black infants are harder to place in foster homes. Besides, according to professor Ricke Solinger, author of *Wake Up Little Susie: Single Pregnancy and Race Before Roe v. Wade*, the black community always has helped in the care of such infants.

Black women, who make up about 6.2 percent of the U.S. population, choose abortion at twice the rate of their white peers (21 per 1,000 for whites, 57 per 1,000 for blacks), according to the Alan Guttmacher Institute.

A lack of funds, transportation and information limit black women's access to abortion services, experts say. LaShunda Jones, an unmarried, pregnant 18-year-old, says she wasn't sure whether abortion was legal. In any case, she decided to carry her unintended pregnancy to term after friends told her the abortion procedure would be physically painful. Some told her abortion was morally wrong. Others said it would jeopardize her ability to conceive in the future.

'I didn't think I was ready to have kids right now, but I knew I was too far along to have an abortion.'

■ ■ ■ ■ ■ ■ ■ ■ ■ ■

"Really, I wasn't planning on keeping this child," says Ms. Jones, hanging her head. "I didn't think I was ready to have kids right now, but I knew I was too far along to have an abortion. I thought it would be easy, but it's not. I guess everything will be all right."

Abortion rights advocates argue that unplanned, unwanted pregnancies force single black women such as Ms. Jones into a dependency on public assistance and other social services. In 1990, the last year for which figures are available, nearly 40 percent of the nation's Aid to Families With Dependent Children recipients were black, according to the U.S. Department of Health and Human Services.

"The explosive growth of out-of-wedlock births and divorces impact our programs far more than any other factor," says Larry Dye, a spokesman for the Administration for Children and Families, a branch of the U.S. Department of Health and Human Services. "It's a frightening trend."

It's one that Catherine, a single, 32-year-old clerical worker, wants no part of. Seven months ago, she used $374 — money for her car and utility bills — to pay for an abortion. She says she barely makes ends meet on her data processor's income and cannot afford to care for a child. She and her former boyfriend had no marriage plans, and she wants a husband when she becomes a mother. Although she hasn't told her conservative Catholic family about the abortion, she says she has no regrets.

"I'm on the pill," she says. "But if I got pregnant again, I'd have another abortion."

August 9, 1992

A Healthy Choice

■ ■ ■ ■ ■ ■ ■ ■ ■ ■

ngie Black consults her daughter before reaching for a cold soda.

"Beverly, do you think one pop would hurt?"

Beverly Williams shakes her head and answers the same way she's answered for the last 15 years.

"Yes, Mama. What happened to the juice I bought you?"

The mother and daughter could be a point-counterpoint commercial for the American Diabetes Association.

Every day, Mrs. Black, who is 70-ish, battles heart disease, diabetes and other chronic ailments. Mrs. Williams, 48, is the very model of fitness; her only medical problem of recent years was the removal of a tiny cyst on her knee caused by rigorous daily workouts.

Clyde W. Yancy Jr., Mrs. Black's physician, says her condition represents the past state of health among African-American women. Mrs. Williams, he says, represents the future.

By almost any measure, African Americans are less healthy than whites. Their average life expectancy is six years shorter. They die more often from preventable or manageable illnesses such as diabetes and heart disease. AIDS is running rampant in many areas: It is the No. 1 killer of young, black women in New York and New Jersey.

During the heyday of the Civil Rights Movement, activists cried for many kinds of freedom: economic parity, integrated education and political empowerment. The issue of African-American health received less attention, perhaps because it is an even more complex problem.

Today, however, some community activists — particularly women — are tackling the problem with vigor, says Evelyn C. White, editor of *Speaking for Ourselves: The Black Women's Health Book.*

African-American communities remain largely matriarchal, with women assuming most of the responsibility for their families' health. African-American women who lead several national health agencies have turned attention to their communities' many medical problems.

More than a decade after the health and fitness craze changed the lifestyles of many white Americans, these African-American women are attacking the historical, educational and economic barriers that have relegated them to the wrong side of wellness.

"We're just sick and tired of being miserable," Ms. White says. "We're actively looking for some kind of guidance, some kind of relief."

Making African Americans healthy will require action on many fronts, activists recognize. It will mean raising the income level of blacks so they can afford medical treatment. It will mean making insurance coverage more widely available. It will mean opening clinics in predominantly black communities for those who cannot or will not travel to established medical centers. It will mean training more African-American doctors, nurses and technicians.

But at an even more basic level, some activists say, improving African Americans' health depends on educating them to take care of themselves, giving them the information that can keep them from damaging their health in the first place. In addition, it means breaking down the fear, distrust and cultural barriers that keep many blacks from using the medical services that already exist.

Making African Americans healthy will require action on many fronts.

Despite its growing national profile, the effort is largely grassroots. Local leaders and ill or recovering community activists drive it. In Dallas, it is manifest in protests against billboards that advertise alcohol and tobacco products.

Pat McKinney, a critical-care nurse at Baylor University Medical Center, spends her free time organizing an annual health fair for the

National Coalition of 100 Black Women. When speaking to medical students at the University of Texas Southwestern Medical School in Dallas, she tells them to be patient with people who speak in ethnic dialects.

"I have a moral responsibility to share my knowledge," Ms. McKinney says. "I want these black people to know how their bodies work. I want them to know that there is preventative care out there. We have to go into the community to teach people. We shouldn't wait until they're sick in the hospital."

Gradually, the message seems to be getting through. Encouraged by television talk-show host Oprah Winfrey's open battle with the bulge, buoyed by Olympic athlete Florence Griffith Joyner's amazing grace, alarmed by the admonitions of U.S. Secretary of Health Louis Sullivan, African-American women are beginning to work on their health as hard as they have worked to support and raise their families.

'We have to go into the community to teach people. We shouldn't wait until they're sick in the hospital.'

■ ■ ■ ■ ■ ■ ■ ■ ■ ■

"The doctor told me to walk forever," Rena Williams says. "I do. We try to keep active."

At 28, Rena Williams (who is not related to Beverly Williams) is slender and energetic. Nothing about her appearance says that she underwent open-heart surgery for a congenital disorder discovered almost a decade ago. Rain or shine, she walks at a park near her suburban Dallas home nearly every day. During the last three years, she says, the number of African-American women pounding the paths has dramatically increased.

"When I started walking in the park, it used to be empty," she says. "Now when I go, the park is filled. Even in the heat of the day, it's filled."

Rena Williams, who is a fast-food restaurant manager, understands the interrelationship of exercise, diet and good health. African Americans have not always had access to information with which to make those connections, says Linda Villarosa, senior editor of *Essence*, a monthly magazine aimed at African-American women. "Health-care messages haven't been targeted toward us," Ms. Villarosa says. "Exercise has been presented as more of a white, middle-class thing. At marathons, for instance, you see thousands of white runners. There aren't many health clubs in our communities. If there are, there are not ones we can afford."

Articles about health get priority at *Essence*, Ms. Villarosa says. A recipe in the August issue substitutes vegetable oil and tomatoes for the smoked meat and salt pork usually used to season collard greens. A feature in the same issue diagrams safe exercises for overweight women and urges them to work their bodies.

"Health writers are just beginning to tell the story of African-American health," says Denise Gary Robinson, president of the Black Health Research Foundation in New York.

Twenty years ago, Angie Black had no way of knowing she was courting high blood pressure, diabetes and heart disease. After her husband died and she became the sole support of her children, she worked a three-job day. She fueled her hectic day with a diet high in Butterfinger candy bars, coffee, fried foods and doughnuts. She rarely went for checkups. Instead she diagnosed and treated her own illnesses with over-the-counter medicines.

The lifestyle took its toll and radicalized her children.

"My mother drank a lot of soda and coffee," Beverly Williams says. "I drink eight to 10 glasses of water every day. I never eat candy. I rarely eat other sweets. I eat a lot of fresh fruits and vegetables."

African-American activists are trying to ensure that information not available to Mrs. Black in years past is available in their communities today. Aiming for average women, Ms. White filled her best-selling book with essays by women recovering from and living with illnesses, as well as analyses by physicians, nurses, leaders and scholars.

"It's for the group of black women lost in the middle, who get little attention," Ms. White says. "There is the underclass, the crack mothers the media focuses on. The other extreme is the Oprahs, the Faye Wattletons who get attention. (Ms. Wattleton is the national director of Planned Parenthood.) This is for the women who go to work and go to school."

Major health organizations also are beginning to tailor their services to African Americans, who may be reluctant to seek treatment at hospitals and clinics out of fear or lack of money. The Dallas chapter of the American Cancer Society, for example, sends a mobile mammography unit to predominantly African-American communities. Two of the brochures stacked outside Dr. Yancy's office feature the faces of African Americans.

Vickie Washington-Nance, who teaches part time at a Dallas high school, says African Americans must become savvy consumers of health care. Her husband's job provides health insurance, but she says that co-payments can be daunting to a family with limited resources.

"I'm a practical person," Mrs. Nance says. "We're in an HMO (health maintenance organization), so office visits are only $10. If they were $40, we wouldn't go."

Mrs. Nance also has just helped organize one of two local groups affiliated with the National Black Women's Health Project, a self-help organization that began in Atlanta and now has 96 chapters nationwide.

Minnie Pryor, a nurse-administrator at the Routh Street Women's Clinic in Dallas, leads the other local group. Members meet monthly to discuss their health needs, their fears, home remedies and their experiences with local health-care providers.

The Atlanta chapter has received grants to open women's clinics at housing projects.

For all the hope such grass-roots efforts engender, medical professionals say they face enormous cultural and economic hurdles.

Dr. Yancy, a cardiologist and assistant professor of medicine at UT Southwestern, says many lower-income people may put off visiting a doctor because they are paid hourly and cannot afford time away from the typewriter or assembly line. He said he has had patients who live in high-crime areas check themselves out of the hospital against orders to get to their mailboxes before thieves steal their Social Security or welfare checks.

By the time many African Americans seek care, their illnesses are advanced. In many cases, fear and suspicion have kept them away.

Hospitals, like other public institutions, have opened their doors to African Americans only in the past three decades. Each February, during African-American History Month, black children hear the story of Charles Drew, the African-American physician who pioneered blood plasma research. He died when a Jim Crow hospital refused to admit him after he suffered injuries in a car accident.

Knowing they had nowhere to seek help for an injury or illness, many African Americans passively lived with disease. Some counted on folk remedies or religion to hasten their healing. Some, like Sammie Louise Fridia, still do.

Mrs. Fridia, 49, is receiving chemotherapy for breast cancer, a disease she insists she doesn't have even though her right breast is three times the size of the left.

"They want to say it's a cancer tumor," Mrs. Fridia says, "but it ain't no cancer tumor."

A fundamentalist Christian, Mrs. Fridia bravely calls her ordeal a "test of faith." Skeptical about the powers of medical science, she attributes many of her symptoms to her treatment.

"The antibiotics are bringing my infection up," she says, spitting into a paper-towel-lined tray. "I didn't feel sick till I started going to the doctor."

She is supplementing her doctor's treatment with a rigorous regimen of prayer and home remedies. A nearly empty bottle of olive oil rests on the table next to her living-room sickbed. The oil was blessed by her preacher, and she rubs it on her scalp, expecting it to restore the hair she has lost as a result of chemotherapy.

Some have passively lived with disease. Some have counted on folk remedies or religion to hasten their healing.

■ ■ ■ ■ ■ ■ ■ ■ ■ ■

Because of a dearth of African-American doctors, blacks who seek care are likely to be treated by white physicians. Although African-American and white doctors have the same training, their backgrounds and manner of approaching patients may differ, says

Dr. Yancy, an African American.

The Black Health Research Foundation, established two years ago in New York, is trying to bring racial balance to the health-care professions. The non-profit organization is patterned after the American Heart Association and other member-driven medical charities. Its health awareness campaign is led by R&B diva Patti LaBelle, who has had several close friends and relatives die from preventable or curable ailments.

The agency provides scholarships to medical students and budding research scientists in hopes of developing a cadre of African-American researchers and health-care professionals. It also funds research on diseases that affect African Americans disproportionately.

Ms. Robinson, the agency's president, visits inner-city grocery stores whenever business takes her across the country. She searches for fresh produce, lean meats and high-fiber and low-calorie foods. If she doesn't find them, she tries to educate the owners through subsequent phone calls and mailings.

Dr. Yancy is heartened by these and other efforts to improve the prognosis for African-American health.

"They are dramatic examples of the direction things should be going in," he says. "You can only tell someone that there's nothing you can do for so long. It's too painful."

July 22, 1990

Her Strong Suit

■ ■ ■ ■ ■ ■ ■ ■ ■ ■

laine Mayes taps her foot to *Somebody Pray for Me*, a gospel tune pulsing out of the living-room radio. She is sprawled across the sofa, snuggling her 6-year-old and explaining why the family's religious beliefs prohibit the girl from wearing a witch Halloween costume.

The conversation, the music, the affection all come after a long day's work, Mrs. Mayes' first in about a year and a half. She says she ran away from a "good" job after fighting a futile battle with the supervisor and corporate officials who ignored her pleas for help over sexual harassment. Family, friends and former colleagues say a male supervisor showered Mrs. Mayes with sexual innuendoes, cut her overtime and humiliated her until she crumbled under three years of daily attacks.

Mrs. Mayes has vowed to tell about the havoc sexual harassment wreaks on victims and their families. After months of therapy, prayer and soul-searching, she decided to speak out and to sue her former employer, Ketema Inc. of Grand Prairie.

Her attorney, Don Peavy Sr. of Fort Worth, filed suit in federal court last week, alleging sexual harassment and seeking unspecified damages.

Mrs. Mayes' former supervisor, Larry Gayton, denies the allegations. The director of Ketema's legal department declined to comment because the matter is in litigation.

Reached by phone at Ketema, a manufacturer of heat exchangers, Mr. Gayton said, "I have no comment, none whatsoever because this litigation has not been closed."

Jesse J. Guin, director of Ketema's legal department, refused to comment on Mrs. Mayes' allegations.

"I would love to be of assistance to you," Mr. Guin said, "but we have a policy not to comment on anything which is in litigation."

Wayne Lee, Dallas lawyer for Mr. Gayton, says Mrs. Mayes sued his client individually earlier this year. Mr. Gayton maintains his innocence; his homeowner's insurance policy settled the case to avoid costly litigation, Mr. Lee says.

"He denies any of the accusations," Mr. Lee says. "The case was settled for a nominal amount. It was settled for a nominal fee to make it go away."

A separate federal lawsuit against Ketema also has been filed. It arose from an Equal Employment Opportunity Commission complaint that Mrs. Mayes filed against Ketema in 1990. A complainant can sue only with the federal commission's approval.

In the EEOC complaint, Mrs. Mayes says, "Since approximately June 1987 to June 1990, I was bothered, tormented, ridiculed and denied transfer by my supervisor, Larry Gayton. He has intimidated me in many areas which ultimately resulted in my physician's request on June 4, 1990, for medical disability leave."

"I am the only female in the department," she says in the complaint. "Larry Gayton does not intimidate the men under his supervison. After I complained about Larry Gayton's harassment of me to higher management, they began to treat me in a negative manner which created a harsh, hostile work environment."

Her numerous complaints to upper management produced no results, Mrs. Mayes says in the EEOC complaint.

Mrs. Mayes, 32, says she took a full-time job with Ketema three years after she graduated from Fort Worth's Polytechnic Senior High School in 1977. Punching the clock at the Grand Prairie factory made the young wife and mother feel more grown-up, more responsible. The added income helped her family buy into the American Dream — a brick, three-bedroom house in the Dallas suburb of Arlington.

As the only female clerk in her section of the plant stockroom, Mrs. Mayes says, she was proud of her spotless work area and her neat inventory of nuts, bolts and gaskets.

"I took my line and gave it the woman's touch," Mrs. Mayes says.

At the end of a yearlong maternity leave in 1985, the mother of two says, she returned to a new supervisor and an expanded stockroom. Her first unhappy encounter with the new boss occurred when she took him lewd drawings and obscene notes that a co-worker had left on her desk.

"He laughed and joked about them," she says. "He put them in a drawer. I don't think he ever referred the problem to personnel."

Within days, Mrs. Mayes says, Mr. Gayton began to stare at her as she worked. He'd stand inches from her for 30 to 40 minutes each day.

"There was no warning," Mrs. Mayes says. "It was so uncomfortable. He'd stand at my desk with his butt in my face. He'd peek at me from beneath the bins. He watched me walk up and down the aisle. He would undress me going, and he'd undress me coming back."

There were several such episodes. After each, she says, she confronted him: "I said, "What do you want?""

His response, Mrs. Mayes says, was always the same: "I want you."

Another colleague, a woman who is still employed by Ketema, says Mr. Gayton interfered with Mrs. Mayes' attempts to train for a position outside the stock area. The woman agreed to speak only if her identity was not revealed.

'He watched me walk up and down the aisle. He would undress me going, and he'd undress me coming back.'

■ ■ ■ ■ ■ ■ ■ ■ ■ ■

"He would pass by the window," the woman says. "He'd return to his office, then call and ask how much longer Elaine would be there. The schedule was set. He knew how long she'd be there. He'd pass by the window and call her name. Her hands would tremble. Her eyes would twitch."

Although Mrs. Mayes says Mr. Gayton never explicitly made sexual favors a condition of her employment, his advances increased in frequency and intensity. He began touching her shoulders when he came to her desk, and he insisted that she sit next to him after he paged her to report to his office, which he did at least three times each day. He rarely discussed work during these frequent meetings, Mrs. Mayes says.

"One time he said, "My mom is in the hospital. There's a black nurse helping her. She's so pretty. She looks just like you. She has eyes just like yours.""

Mrs. Mayes says a few of her colleagues noted Mr. Gayton's behavior and began to accompany her to his office to work on the computer while he spoke with her.

A former colleague, a man, stated in an affidavit, "He (Mr. Gayton) has even told me to stay away from her — that she was 'off limits.'"

Mrs. Mayes says she complained to the plant manager, a vice president and others, to no avail.

"I told his immediate supervisor," she says. "That was a big step for me. He looked at me and grinned. He said, "What are you saying, Elaine, that he wants your body?""

Mr. Gayton retaliated, she says. He refused to schedule her for overtime. He moved her desk behind a large table saw.

"Whenever a forklift drove by, and they drove by all day," says Mrs. Mayes, her eyes filling with tears, "the sawdust would blow in my face. All my papers would blow to the floor.

"He would wait for me outside the restroom," Mrs. Mayes continues. "He was like a fly you had to keep swatting away. My mama thought it would turn into one of those fatal attraction things."

> **Mrs. Mayes insists that she isn't being dramatic when she says his actions nearly killed her.**
>
> ▪ ▪ ▪ ▪ ▪ ▪ ▪ ▪ ▪ ▪

Mrs. Mayes insists that she isn't being dramatic when she says Mr. Gayton's actions nearly killed her. She motions toward a thick stack of medical documents piled on her living-room coffee table in which doctors' notes describe her stress-related conditions.

Her thick, long hair, once a source of pride, came out in clumps, she says. A psychiatrist's diagnosis was depression, and Prozac was prescribed. Her eyes developed a chronic stress-related twitch called myokymia. The toll, says the Rev. R.E. West, pastor of Greater

Strangers Rest Baptist Church, is obvious.

"Elaine was an attractive young lady," Mr. West says. "After this thing started at work, she gained quite a bit of weight."

Mr. West, the family's minister for almost 13 years, says he first thought his parishioner's reaction was extreme. Then he realized that nothing in Mrs. Mayes' experience had prepared her to cope with anyone who mistreated her.

"Elaine's been in a bubble-type environment," Mr. West says. "She started dating her husband in high school. From high school on, it was just Elaine and Renick (Mr. Mayes). She never had experiences with other men. She's a little naive. A little gullible."

Dr. Linda Webb-Watson, a Dallas psychotherapist who has advised an area sexual-harassment support group, says Mrs. Mayes' reaction isn't extreme. The response of women harassed by supervisors depends on what Dr. Webb-Watson calls "preconditioning."

"It depends on her views," Dr. Webb-Watson says. "If she only thought of herself as an American, as an individual rewarded for hard work and loyalty, then it's likely that she would experience disorientation when she finds out she has partial rights and privileges.

"Sexual harassment is very difficult because a woman's identity is destroyed," Dr. Webb-Watson adds. "She is alienated. It can lead to depression."

The EEOC received 5,694 complaints of sexual harassment in 1990, a number that one labor economist says does not reflect the number of women who experience sexual harassment on the job. Julianne Malveaux of San Francisco says most women find the cost of complaining greater than potential remedies.

"The cases are very hard to report," Dr. Malveaux says. "A third of all women are clerical workers. They don't have the wherewithal to complain. They don't have the professional credentials to move.

"One-third of all women, regardless of race, are in poverty because of women's wages," Dr. Malveaux says. "Women don't have the luxury to complain. For every woman who complains, there are 10 who don't."

As a child, Mrs. Mayes attached herself to the Baptist church, becoming the kind of member ministers love to count among their flock. A self-described born-again Christian, Mrs. Mayes sings tenor in the choir, visits the sick and imprisoned and helps coordinate two women's committees at Greater Strangers Rest.

"I counsel Christian teens," Mrs. Mayes says. "I'm also president of the outreach mission."

She's a woman who starts a lot of sentences with, "If it's the Lord's will..." She punctuates other statements with, "This is America," and, "We're average, hard-working Americans." A weathered Desert Storm sticker is stuck to the rear bumper of her brown 1985 Cavalier.

Before the ordeal, Mrs. Mayes says, she was also a doting mother who hung out at the local mall, window shopping and buying costume jewelry for her daughters. The family's days ended on a sour note unless she ate dinner with Kendra, 13, and Ty.

"We would go to the movies," Mrs. Mayes says. "We'd hop in the car and go visit. We just sat in the floor and listened to gospel (music). On Wednesday, we went to youth church for the kids."

The routine unwound when she returned to work in 1985 after giving birth to Ty. It was then, says Renick, Elaine's husband of 14 years, that his sweet-tempered wife turned into an ill-tempered, sickly stranger.

"She was always in a bad mood," Mr. Mayes says. "She never had no energy. I had to come home after working 12 or 14 hours and take care of the girls by myself. I fixed dinner. I helped them with their homework."

In the old days, Mr. Mayes says, his wife "used to get off work, pick up the kids, then we would have dinner like a normal family. My wife was a very outgoing person. She tried to treat everyone right. She loves the Lord.

"What he did to her was like taking two wheels off a car," Mr. Mayes says. "It still runs, but it's bumpy. How would you like to come home to a wife who's not your wife?"

Mr. Mayes says he begged Elaine to quit. She refused.

"She said, "Renick, why should I have to go?"

"I worked because I had to work," Mrs. Mayes says. "I have a sick child. My oldest daughter is a severe asthmatic. Her medicine is very expensive."

Even today, the suggestion of quitting angers Mrs. Mayes. Her voice becomes stern, almost strident as she explains why she didn't leave sooner. She says that because her upbringing had taught her to respect authority and use "the system," she hoped that one of the several company officials to whom she complained would intervene as they had promised.

"There's a company policy book that says if you have a problem, go to management," Mrs. Mayes says. "I did!"

Also, she says, because she had spent her entire career at Ketema, she was reluctant to give up the benefits and security she'd earned in 10 years of employment.

"I'd just gotten my fourth week of vacation," Mrs. Mayes says. "I was making good money. Why should I have quit and started at the bottom someplace else?

"If I had been there 90 days, I would have quit," Mrs. Mayes says. "If I'd been there 18 months, I would have quit. The real issue is that I had to work for a living. Why should I have to quit when all the company had to do was educate him?"

As of March 30, 1989, the company had a sexual harassment policy, which was posted on the bulletin board. The memo defines sexual harassment and says it is considered a major offense that can result in disciplinary action, including discharge. The policy statement encourages employees to report sexual harassment to management and promises that such reports will be investigated.

Mr. Guin, Ketema's director of legal services, declined to comment on the company's current sexual harassment policy or to provide a copy.

'The real issue is that I had to work for a living. Why should I have to quit when all the company had to do was educate him?'

■ ■ ■ ■ ■ ■ ■ ■ ■ ■

Kendra Mayes, a gangly teenager who plays basketball for Kennedale Junior High, says the mother she'd always counted on gradually disappeared.

"My friends would come over, and she'd be rude to them,"

Kendra says. "They stopped coming over. If I tried to talk about my day (at school), she'd say, 'Let me clear my head.' She'd call us to the (dinner) table, but nobody would say anything 'til she started to talk. Then we knew it was OK to speak."

Mrs. Mayes started having panic attacks at the grocery store and in other public places.

"All of a sudden, she would start breathing funny," Kendra says. "I thought she was having a heart attack. It hurt so bad. I asked Daddy, 'Why is she going crazy?'"

Even her church family noticed the change.

"It got to the point that whenever she would speak in church, the topic would be men," Mr. West says. "She'd speak in a condemning tone. She'd tell the women, 'Watch these men. They're nothing but Satan. They can have a family, and they'll still come at you.' Members would ask, "What's wrong with Elaine? Why does she keep bringing up men?'"

Mrs. Mayes recalls munching a pickle while sitting at a traffic light one day. A man pulled up beside her and asked for a bite.

"I chased him through four lights," she says.

More painful than the harassment was the devastating impact it had on family finances.

■ ■ ■ ■ ■ ■ ■ ■ ■ ■

More painful than the harassment was the devastating impact it had on family finances, Mrs. Mayes says. When she went on disability leave, the family had trouble making the mortgage payment. She quit Ketema when the disability ran out. A roof leak destroyed Ty's bed early this year, and it remains unrepaired.

"Sexual harassment doesn't just happen to the woman," Mrs. Mayes says. "We've done without so much around here: clothes for the kids. The lights have been cut off. The phone. An (emergency) medical bracelet for my daughter. It affects the whole family."

The damage, however, doesn't have to be lifelong. She snapped out of despair the day she decided she could solve her problem by killing her boss.

"I was ready to kill him," she remembers. "I'd been looking at guns. Talk about full of hell and upset, I was going to wipe them all out. The only thing that prevented a bloodbath was the fact that I didn't own a gun."

The anger galvanized Mrs. Mayes. She called lawyers. She contacted the National Organization for Women, which sponsors a Dallas-Fort Worth area sexual harassment support group. Her physician recommended a therapist. She pitched her story to Robert Ashley, host of *Community Forum*, a daily talk show on a Christian radio station. She also appeared on *Reporters' Round Table*, a weekly radio show on a station that targets black listeners.

"I want men to know, 'Hands off,'" Mrs. Mayes says. "I want men to know that when a woman says, no, it's NO! I want men to know that if they're not going to squeeze other men's breasts or pop their bra straps, then they shouldn't do it to women."

Although she says her recovery is far from complete, Mrs. Mayes measures her progress in displays of courage. After getting clearance from her doctors last month, she signed up with a temporary employment agency.

Kendra is delighted to finally have a mother again.

"It's taken her a humongous, long time to get back to herself," Kendra says. "Maybe we'll even get to go to the mall."

November 10, 1991

EPILOGUE: Elaine Mayes eventually settled her case against Ketema Inc. out of court for a modest amount. It was time, she said, "to get on with life." If anything, the newspaper article, she said, "granted me great justice." After two years of temp work, she began work on March 7, 1994, as an administrative technician at the Texas Department of Human Resources. She was delighted to discover she would be supervised by a woman.

SECTION IX

·

BLOOD
SISTERS

···········

Rite or Wrong?

■ ■ ■ ■ ■ ■ ■ ■ ■ ■

PARIS — Aminata Diop lay awake the night before she was to begin her ritual passage to womanhood. Before dawn, she rose and walked out the door of her family's mud house in Sikasso, a farming village in southern Mali.

Those steps eventually carried her to France — and into a lonely and unfamiliar new world where the intimate details of her life are the subject of government deliberations and feminist debates.

Her sad 23-year-old face reflects the burden of ancient tradition. Her shoulders droop with the consequences of her actions.

From the day 29 months ago when she refused a ritual circumcision — the removal of her clitoris and inner labia, performed without sterilization or anesthesia — Ms. Diop has hovered in an abyss between tribal tradition and the Western idea of individual choice.

There is little for her to do as she awaits the outcome of an international campaign to win her political asylum, a goal pressed by feminists such as Renee Boutet de Monvel, the 74-year-old Parisian gynecologist who took her in.

She hovers in an abyss between tribal tradition and the Western ideal of individual choice.

■ ■ ■ ■ ■ ■ ■ ■ ■ ■

"I attend French classes all day," Ms. Diop says. "I watch TV and I sleep a great deal."

Occasionally, Marie-Helene Franjou, another French benefactor, invites her over for a game of cards. But Ms. Diop's schedule provides plenty of time for worry. Mainly, she worries about the fate of her mother, an unskilled, illiterate woman who was abandoned by her father as punishment for Aminata's defiance.

"My father told my mother: 'Your daughter is dirty and bad-spirited,'" Ms. Diop says. "Only a bad mother could raise a bad daughter."

She also frets about her own future, says Linda Weil-Curiel, Ms. Diop's lawyer: where she will live if Dr. Monvel should die; if she will marry; how many times she will have to retell her story.

"Aminata was completely paralyzed when the (refugee) commission asked her to explain what happened in Africa," Ms. Weil-Curiel says. "The pain, it does not diminish. She relives it each time she must recount the tragedy."

The only thing that doesn't worry Ms. Diop is whether French officials will send her back to Mali. Her lawyer and other advocates helped her obtain a *carte de sejour* and a *carte de travail*, roughly the equivalent of a green card in the United States. Although she has twice been denied political asylum, the documents allow her to remain in France for as long as she wants.

Her mother and sisters dodged her questions, and she could find no literature to explain the procedure.

■ ■ ■ ■ ■ ■ ■ ■ ■ ■

Although millions of women around the world have been circumcised, including virtually all the women in rural Mali, Ms. Diop had to fight for information about the surgery she was expected to undergo. Her mother and sisters dodged her earliest questions, and she could find no literature to explain the procedure.

Her family is Muslim, and among many Muslim women, sexuality remains an intensely personal topic, says a Malian professional woman who lives in Virginia. The woman, a 29-year-old electrical engineer, did not have a clitoridectomy. She doesn't know whether her mother, a midwife, had the procedure.

"I would never ask," the woman says. "That is a personal question."

In Ms. Diop's native language, Bambara, villagers use the word *bolokolu*, or "washing of hands," to describe clitoridectomy. A female ironsmith uses a crude instrument to remove the clitoris and inner labia. Girls who get sick or die are thought to be invaded by spirits. The ancient rite ends with a feast — a celebration that many newly circumcised girls are too weak to attend.

"They beat tom-toms, and there is singing and dancing," Ms. Diop says. "The girls do not talk about what happens. They do not smile. After asking, I knew something would be cut off."

She learned more after she left home at age 12 to attend school in Bamako, the capital city. There, her circumcised classmates divulged some details.

"Old ladies from the village hold your legs and a matron cuts you," she says. "Sometimes a woman has to sit on your belly to hold you down because it is so painful."

Their stories, and the death of her best friend, who died a few days after being circumcised, terrified her.

"She died Sept. 24, 1989," Ms. Diop says. "I will never forget that. I cried for three days."

Female circumcision is an ancient custom currently practiced by a multitude of African, Arab and Asian societies. World Health Organization officials estimate that between 75 million and 85 million women worldwide have had the procedure. Although pervasive in some nations where Islam dominates, it is considered a cultural rather than religious practice, says Ellen Gruenbaum, an anthropology professor at California State University in San Bernadino.

Explanations for female circumcision vary from culture to culture. Depending on where it is done, it is considered moral, hygienic, social or aesthetic.

Many cultures believe that children have androgynous genitalia. Removing the foreskin from a penis or the clitoris from the vagina is thought to make the individual more masculine or feminine, says Janice Boddy, a University of Toronto anthropologist who has conducted extensive field research on the subject. Another goal, one feminists find objectionable, is thought to be the reduction of female sexual desire.

"To us, it looks barbaric," says Jean Camaroff, an anthropology professor at the University of Chicago. "Westerners are quick to be pejorative. But women in nations where this is done by and large are not in revolt against this."

In Ms. Diop's tribe, couples do not marry without being circumcised. And almost without exception, women eventually marry. When she was 8, Ms. Diop's parents promised her to the son of her father's best friend. As her wedding day drew near, the family planned her clitoridectomy. Dreading the pain and fearing for her life, she pleaded for exemption.

"The ceremony was decided," Ms. Diop says. "I asked my fiance if he would marry me without it. He said I must have it. I begged my father to spare me. He beat me."

Her clitoridectomy was scheduled to follow Ramadan, Islamic holy days observed with prayer and dawn-to-dusk fasting. The day of the ceremony, Ms. Diop woke before dawn and slipped out of her father's house.

"I walked for my life," she says.

'I begged my father to spare me. He beat me.'

■ ■ ■ ■ ■ ■ ■ ■ ■ ■

She trudged 30 miles before hitching a ride with a trucker, who dropped her off at her aunt's house in Bamako. When she explained why she had run away, her aunt threw her out. She turned to her peers. They criticized and shunned her. "They said they would be ashamed to be with me," says Ms. Diop, shifting in her chair.

Finally, a family friend who worked for a Belgian airline used her connections to secure a passport for Ms. Diop and arrange a one-way ticket to Brussels, Belgium. From there, the fugitive got a ride to Paris, where she knew a Malian couple.

Leaving Mali was Ms. Diop's only choice, says Dr. Gruenbaum, the Cal State anthropologist. "The amount of help she would have found would have been limited," she says. "Your personal honor is tied to family relationships. If you defy your family, you lose everything."

Having lost so much, Ms. Diop says she is still glad to have put female circumcision in the international spotlight.

Her story has intrigued the press and rallied feminists. European magazines and newspapers have chronicled the case. And over the past few months, American publications such as *Glamour* and *The Washington Post* have mentioned Ms. Diop in their coverage of women's issues. *Ms. Magazine* asked readers to send French government officials letters protesting the decision to deny Ms. Diop political asylum.

"It is useful to spread out the knowledge that such a practice exists, and it must be fought," says Ms. Diop. "I would like to help women in my country free themselves from the harmful practices."

Whether all of them want to be freed is another matter. Some African women — highly educated, well-traveled professional women who now live in Western countries — oppose circumcision. Others don't.

A secretary at the Mali embassy in Washington who had a clitoridectomy says many of her peers see the custom in the same way Westerners see baptisms. "It's not a crime," the secretary says. "It is traditional. I had one done. I'm all right." However, if she had a daughter, she says, she would not force the girl to undergo the procedure.

The Virginia engineer similarly believes that clitoridectomies should not be mandatory, but neither should they be banned. "Women should be able to choose," she says.

The debate, simmering now for more than a decade, often pits Western women against women from developing nations, anthropologists say. Westerners struggle to understand what they view as submissive behavior; non-Western women struggle to understand what they view as cultural imperialism.

"This practice just keeps women in their place," says Ms. Weil-Curiel, the French lawyer and feminist.

"There is poverty throughout Africa," says the Malian engineer who lives in Virginia. "There are health problems, food shortages and many more pressing concerns. Why is this so important?"

The World Health Organization has urged governments to outlaw female circumcision and to develop educational programs describing the health risks. However, although it is banned in the Sudan, Burkina Faso and Kenya, it persists in those countries, anthropologists say.

In France, feminist lawyers and some prosecutors have begun to vigorously pursue immigrants and others who perform clitoridectomies there. In view of those prosecutions, Ms. Weil-Curiel finds it ironic that the French government has refused to grant Ms. Diop political asylum. On principle, she vows to continue the fight.

However, Victoria Butler, a spokeswoman from the United Nations High Commission on Refugees, says Ms. Diop failed to fit the Geneva Convention's definition of a refugee in one critical respect.

"Her persecutor was not the government," but rather her family, Ms. Butler says.

Perched on the edge of a stuffed chair in her lawyer's office, Ms. Diop says that neither a government nor a family has the right to persecute an individual — the right to force a woman to do something against her will.

"Women must be strong," she says.

Surrounded by law books and French country antiques, this round-faced, soft-spoken woman seems as out of place as she must feel. Her clothes, donated discards, are far from chic. Malian rhythms still accent her imperfect French.

But she is adjusting.

The Metro, Paris' complex and efficient subway, is fine. Having few friends in Paris is not. She misses the closeness she shared with her fiance back home, and she has found no romantic interest in France.

"African men don't want me," she says, sighing.

Nonetheless, an independent woman is emerging. The French government provides her about $260 a month in *chomage*, a subsidy similar to unemployment. She picks up other money cleaning offices. For the first time, she spends money the way she wants to.

"I am proud of what I have done," she says. "I feel free."

March 2, 1992

Dallas Morning News staff writer Mark McDonald also contributed to this report.

Scarred by Tradition

■ ■ ■ ■ ■ ■ ■ ■ ■ ■

MERU, Kenya — Agnes Manyara's smooth, kidney bean-colored complexion is interrupted by a row of tiny, barely visible tribal markings etched beneath each eye. They are beauty marks, she explains. Not scars.

The scars, says the agricultural agent, are between her legs. Shiny keloids crisscross the otherwise soft tissue of her vulva. The scars formed more than two years ago, soon after her mother-in-law, her sister-in-law and several of her husband's other female relatives held Mrs. Manyara down while a woman she'd never met used a dirty knife to cut off her clitoris and part of her inner labia.

"I screamed," she says quietly. "No one came to my aid."

The genital mutilation changed Mrs. Manyara, but not the way the age-old practice is intended to transform the estimated 2 million African girls and women on whom it is performed each year.

For centuries, it has been performed as a rite of passage, a ceremonial ritual marking a girl's transition into womanhood. But in the past decade, as African countries have become more developed and African women more educated, attitudes have begun to shift.

Today, a growing segment of the African population looks on the procedure as brutal mutilation.

■ ■ ■ ■ ■ ■ ■ ■ ■ ■

Today, a growing segment of the African population looks on the procedure not as a revered cultural expression but as brutal mutilation with serious physical and emotional consequences. Mrs. Manyara's self-esteem was sacrificed, and she suffered physical injuries.

In the 25 African nations where female circumcision is common, the procedure is at the symbolic core of women's traditional role in society. It is the starting point of a labyrinth of customs that in practice destine women to a life of hard labor, compulsory pregnancies, spousal abuse, illiteracy and serious health problems.

Among African men and women, misogyny is couched in terms of culture and tradition, says Donna Pido, an American anthropologist who has lived in Kenya since the mid-1960s. "They say, 'This is the African way.'"

■ Millions affected

In Africa, female circumcision — or as its critics call it, female genital mutilation — is most prevalent among nations that border the Nile and Niger rivers.

About half of Kenya's estimated 12.5 million women and girls have undergone the procedure. In Somalia, the incidence is as high as 90 percent; in Mali, 75 percent.

In all, 100 million women and girls around the world have been circumcised, according to estimates by the World Health Organization. Experts also say the practice is on the rise where Africans have migrated — developed nations including the United States, France, Canada, Italy and Britain.

Female genital mutilation is prohibited or officially condemned in most of the African countries where it is routinely performed. The Kenyan government outlawed the practice in 1982. But in the face of centuries-old social custom, laws are ignored and rarely enforced.

"The government is aware of the practice but has done little to prevent it and less to punish practitioners," says Lorna Mbugua, Nairobi spokeswoman for an international health organization based in Washington.

In February her group, the Program for Appropriate Technology in Health, released a study showing that female genital mutilation is so common that some health-care workers — even doctors who have taken the Hippocratic Oath, swearing to do no harm — moonlight as "excisionists."

The procedure can be minor — a simple nick across the hood of the clitoris. Or it can be severe. In a method called "infibulation," the clitoris, inner labia and most of the soft flesh of the labia majora are scraped or cut away. The two sides of the vulva then are fastened together with acacia thorns, catgut or a glue made from sticky herbs or eggs. During the recovery process, which can take several weeks, girls' hips and legs are bound together to keep the wound from reopening. A hole smaller than a lentil is left to allow the passage of urine and menstrual fluid.

The age of initiates varies among the many cultures and countries where genital mutilation is practiced. In Kenya, girls between ages 10 and 15 are circumcised. Infant girls between the seventh and 40th day of life are circumcised in some Ethiopian areas. Nigerian toddlers undergo the procedure. Among a handful of tribes, it is performed on elderly women.

As initiates' mothers held the little girls' legs, women sang songs about womanhood and danced in the early morning light.

Tradition requires that girls remain silent during the cutting, which usually takes place on the ground without anesthetic. A special dagger, customarily passed down through generations of excisionists, is used on every girl initiated during the same ceremony. The use of one dagger raises the specter of AIDS.

Increasing opposition is modernizing the procedure in many places. During a February rite in Belet Amin, Somalia, a traditional birth attendant injected five 8- to 10-year-old girls with Novocain. The attendant, 50-year-old Cosobo Noor, then circumcised each girl with a separate, sterile razor. As the initiates' mothers held the little girls' legs, women sang songs about womanhood and danced in the early morning light.

Traditionalists who compare female circumcision to its male counterpart don't know the facts, says Rosemary Mburu, a Nairobi gynecologist who has researched the subject. Unlike male circumci-

221

sion, where the foreskin of the penis is removed, the female procedure results in far more than a cosmetic and hygenic change.

"Boys are circumcised," Dr. Mburu says. "Girls are mutilated.
No one would disagree if they saw the problems we must try to solve
in the hospitals."

In Kenya, at least 15 percent of the women and girls who are circumcised die from bleeding or infection, Ms. Mbugua says. In the
Sudan, an estimated one-third of all girls who live in areas where antibiotics are unavailable die from complications.

Human rights lawyer Seble Dawitt wants the United Nations to
oppose female genital mutilation along with other human rights violations.

"There should no longer be any question that this is a violation
of bodily integrity, the right to health, freedom from discrimination,
children's rights and right to life," says Ms. Dawitt, an Ethiopian
who was circumcised as an infant. "Much of the failure to act has to
do with the inscrutability of the family."

■ No warning

Agnes Manyara is now 37. She was attacked by her in-laws two
years ago while her husband was in Nairobi.

"They dragged me across the ground," Mrs. Manyara says.
"Someone put her hand over my mouth and pinched my nose. At
first I tried to fight, but there were too many."

There was no warning. She had no earlier indication that her in-
laws felt so strongly about circumcision. The subject didn't come up
during marriage negotiations. Her husband, Christopher Manyara,
had purposely sought out a mate who had not undergone the
surgery.

Mr. Manyara, a balding, studious-looking teacher, says he knew
his mother and sister were circumcised, but he wanted a wife who
wasn't.

"The traditional women in my village were submissive," says Mr.
Manyara, who is 40. "I like a woman who is straightforward."

A trusted college biology teacher had described to Mr. Manyara
the harmful effects of genital mutilation.

"I developed a negative attitude toward it," he says.

In Agnes, Mr. Manyara found a woman who was raised to be independent. Born into a modern Protestant family of farmers, she was a ninth-grade dropout. But she later enrolled in a vocational school. She met Mr. Manyara in Meru, where both had gone to work.

Circumcision, and all the customs that went with it, were never part of her upbringing. But when she married, she met many of the traditional expectations for Kenyan wives.

She moved to Munithu to live among her husband's relatives, as custom dictates. She learned to prepare his meals the way his mother had. She learned to keep her small house the way his mother kept hers.

Some of her other routines, though, were less traditional for rural women. She held a part-time job that took her, three or four days a week, to teach male landowners techniques to prevent soil erosion on their tiny fruit and vegetable farms or their sizable hillside tea and coffee plantations.

When she married, she met many of the traditional expectations for Kenyan wives.

Rather than encourage her enterprise, her husband's relatives derided her independence. They spread rumors that she was selling sex to area farmers.

"They always changed when Christopher left for school," Mrs. Manyara says. "They would boss me. They were unkind. They said, 'She went to town, she prostituted herself.'

"Not true," she says. "I had no one to be by my side."

Like many other Kenyan men, Mr. Manyara was working and living apart from his family. Five days a week, he was teaching at St. Lucy's, a boarding school for blind girls, a 90-minute bus ride from Munithu.

That left his wife and their four children to depend on his family for support. Friday nights, he came home for the weekend.

Eight years into the marriage, Mrs. Manyara's sister-in-law

knocked on the door. Within moments, Mrs. Manyara was held down on the living room floor and circumcised. Her children were sleeping in the next room.

Afterward, she made her way to bed, squeezing her thighs together to stop the bleeding, listening to the radio in a futile attempt to forget the pain of the injuries she had suffered as she fought against her assailants — a dislocated shoulder, a swollen arm, a bruised mouth.

A half-hour later, her sister-in-law returned, and without uttering a word, offered Mrs. Manyara a cup of tea.

■ Daughter and wife

Traditionally in Kenya, women have had two roles: daughter and wife. Genital mutilation provided the connection between the two. Because the procedure reduces a girl's sexual desire and makes intercourse painful, families believe that a girl will be less likely to experiment sexually before marriage. Virginity guarantees a higher bride price or dowry during nuptial negotiations.

"A mother's duty is to make sure her daughter marries well," says Ms. Mbugua of the Program for Appropriate Technology in Health. "But many men refuse to marry a girl who is not circumcised. An African woman has no status unless she is married."

Marriage offers financial security for Kenyan women, but it comes at a steep price.

Kenyan women traditionally work longer and harder than men. Although the women may labor as long as 18 hours a day, it's common to see men in more relaxed settings on weekdays — chatting over cups of tea or lingering over a newspaper.

Kenyan women are often too exhausted or too busy to eat properly or visit a doctor when they or their children become ill.

"They almost work themselves to death," says Francesta Farmer, an African-American lawyer and project analyst at the Pathfinder Fund, an international nonprofit family-planning agency with offices in Nairobi.

"And if she earns an income," Ms. Farmer says, "she turns it over to her husband. He decides how the money will be spent."

If a married woman does dare to assert herself, she risks being beaten. She also risks being abandoned — a desperate circumstance in a country that has few social services and no shelter system.

A late-1980s survey of 400 women in western Kenya showed that almost 45 percent believed that men have the right to "discipline" their wives.

Such attitudes spill over into other types of violence against girls and women. In July 1991, 71 girls were raped and 19 others killed by male classmates at a coed boarding school in Kenya. Male school officials casually dismissed the rapes, telling investigators that the boys didn't mean to harm the girls, even suggesting that rapes were commonplace at coed high schools. Of 30 boys charged with manslaughter, four were sentenced to prison. None was convicted of rape.

The mass attack at St. Kizito school served as a catalyst for the growing movement against violence toward women.

■ Getting treatment

Agnes Manyara's in-laws kept her closeted in her home, hoping that she would recover from her wounds before her husband's return. But they couldn't stop the rumors, which even reached her parents in Embu, an agricultural center 50 miles south of Meru.

Stories of the attack reached Jackson Kibeteru, the district's constable. He drove to Munithu a week later and questioned residents about Mrs. Manyara.

"The mother-in-law said she didn't know where Agnes was," Mr. Kibeteru says. "She said she thought Agnes had gone to work around Meru; I assessed from her nervousness that she wasn't telling the truth."

A boy told Mr. Kibeteru that the in-laws were holding Mrs. Manyara captive in her bedroom. Fearing that her injuries could prove fatal, Mr. Kibeteru dashed into the house before the in-laws could move Mrs. Manyara.

"If she died, I would be feeling very badly and God would not forgive me," he says. "I wanted to care for her health. I had heard that it was not done in a hygienic way. I wanted Agnes to feel as if she was secure."

Mr. Kibeteru offered to bring his car to the house to take Mrs. Manyara to the hospital in Meru. She decided to walk down the road with him to the car.

"If he left me, they might hurt me again," she says.

Mrs. Manyara's legs, muscular from farm work and carrying children up and down the foothills of Mount Kenya, barely supported her as she hobbled to the chief's car in the chilly winter wind. At the hospital, the staff treated her infection with antibiotics and washed her wounds in warm sitz baths.

"They were very sympathetic," Mrs. Manyara says.

When Mr. Manyara returned, he found his wife in the hospital and his mother and sister in jail. A cousin of his wife was minding the children.

Mr. Kibeteru filed charges against the women. Mrs. Manyara had refused, for fear of retaliation.

The women eventually received probationary sentences. The excisionist was never arrested.

Mr. Kibeteru, 49, doesn't regret pressing the case.

"I'm one of the older men, but I have to change with the times," he says. "If you don't change, you'll be behind everyone else."

■ Growing awareness

Across Kenya, the medical and psychological implications of female genital mutilation are quietly being raised by individuals and groups. Doctors have long known that genital mutilation can cause health problems.

Dr. Mburu, the Nairobi gynecologist, decided to research genital mutilation after treating a woman who suffered from severe depression. After a crude operation, a fissure had developed between the woman's bladder and vagina, and urine trickled down her leg.

"No one wanted to be her friend, and she was very sad," Dr. Mburu says. Genital mutilation complicates childbirth, says Michelle Kelly, a nurse who manages the International Medical Corps' compound in Belet Huen, Somalia.

"The second stage of labor is delayed," Ms. Kelly says. "The baby can't move down the vaginal canal because the scar tissue won't stretch. Infibulated women always need episiotomies. But you must cut up, which means you risk cutting the urethra."

The majority of African women live in rural areas where Caesarean-section technology and trained personnel are not available. The more babies a woman delivers, the more scar tissue she develops, and the more difficult successive births become.

"Women look like hell," Ms. Kelly says. "They are just ripped from stem to stern."

Although there is no formal research to substantiate the anecdotal evidence, Dr. Mburu and other opponents are convinced that genital mutilation contributes to Kenya's high maternal death rate.

She is also convinced that the death rates from cervical cancer and other diseases of the reproductive system are high because gynecological examinations are difficult.

"These poor women are hard to catheterize," she says. "Even finding the vaginal opening is incredibly hard."

Florence W. Manguyu, a Nairobi pediatrician who heads the Medical Women's International Association, says there is a possibility that the practice contributes to a high rate of HIV infection among Kenyan women ages 15 to 25.

'Women look like hell. They are just ripped from stem to stern.'

The Kenyan government has yet to conduct a nationwide study of HIV infection and AIDS rates. Dr. Manguyu bases her figures on AIDS-related deaths and HIV-infected people who seek treatment in clinics and hospitals.

One of the most devastating results of genital mutilation is infertility, says Eddah Gachukia, past president of the African Women Development and Communication Network.

"Africa is very unkind to women who are infertile," Dr. Gachukia says. "Large families indicate prosperity and enhance a man's masculinity."

Genital mutilation changes a girl's behavior as well as her body.

Girls believe that they are adults and often drop out of school by their early teens — a crucial decision in a country that offers no vocational or alternative diploma programs. Girls marry at 13 or 14 and immediately begin having babies, limiting their opportunities and those of their children.

▪ Women protest

Kenyan women have only recently begun to denounce the violence that permeates their lives. Like their Western counterparts, they are confronting these issues through grass-roots organizations and at the ballot box.

When President Daniel arap Moi lifted the legal ban on opposition parties in late 1991, Kenyan women immediately began forming organizations dedicated to ending the political, social and economic oppression of women.

By the end of 1992, a handful of women had been elected to Parliament. While male candidates debated corruption in the ruling party, women focused their campaigns on food, water and medicine shortages, erratic school fees and violence against women.

The victories, though meager, have invigorated women. Still, change that will improve the quality of life for women and girls in Kenya will take considerable time, says Oki Ooko-Ombaka, co-editor of the book, *Women and Law in Kenya: Perspectives and Emerging Issues*. A member of Parliament, he also directs the Kenya Public Law Institute.

"Women must politicize the issues in a way that their male colleagues empathize with them," Mr. Ombaka says. "They (the men) must be persuaded that the concerns of women are the concerns of all Kenyans."

Genital mutilation is increasingly being used as a weapon against women who exercise their independence, Agnes Ndeti, a member of Parliament says.

Parliament member Paul Chepko recently threatened to have Wangari Maathai, Kenya's most outspoken environmental activist, circumcised if she set foot in the Rift Valley again. Since the threat, Ms. Maathai has gone underground.

And during a campaign appearance last fall, parliamentary candidate Nicholas Biwott tried to dissuade voters from supporting his opponent, Tabitha Seii, because she was uncircumcised.

"He said, 'You are a child,'" Mrs. Seii recalls. "He told the voters, 'We've run out of men, and now you are trying to elect a child.'"

Mrs. Seii, 46, says she was stunned that something so personal would become a political issue. She was even more shocked when a group of older women urged her to undergo the procedure.

"For them, the fact that I am not circumcised made me less mature, less able to make informed decisions, less able to represent them in Parliament," she says.

She was soundly defeated by Mr. Biwott, who outspent Mrs. Seii. He was able to convince voters that she wasn't mature enough to represent them.

Although President Moi has strongly condemned violence toward women, especially incest, rape, murder and genital mutilation, many members of Parliament agree that there has been little effort to enforce his position. In September 1982, Mr. Moi took steps to ban the practice after 14 girls died as a result of circumcision. Criticism by women's organizations has motivated no new official initiatives.

Part of the reason, says Dr. Gachukia, is that independent Kenya's most beloved president never pressed the circumcision issue. She holds the late President Jomo Kenyatta partly responsible.

Facing Mount Kenya, Mr. Kenyatta's landmark 1938 work, treats male and female initiation rites with great reverence.

> **'For them, the fact that I am not circumcised made me less mature, less able to make informed decisions. '**
>
> ■ ■ ■ ■ ■ ■ ■ ■ ■ ■ ■

Colonialists opposed circumcision, and Mr. Kenyatta tried, through his book, to explain the procedure's exalted role in Kenyan culture.

"In *Facing Mount Kenya*, Mr. Kenyatta said that one of the purposes of female genital mutilation was to introduce young people to marriage, sex and family life," Dr. Gachukia says. "He also indicated that women were expected to be submissive. The book never acknowledged that genital mutilation was and is deliberately calculated to place women at a disadvantage."

Even now, not everyone embraces the new way of thinking.

Esther Kainda, a former excisionist who lives in a dank one-room cottage on the side of a hill near Meru, can't understand the sudden opposition to traditional practices — especially the one that once helped her earn a living.

In neighboring Somalia, Jaffer, 29, a translator who lives in Belet Huen, couldn't agree more. He says the procedure keeps women from becoming "loose."

"Most Somali parents are for (infibulation) so girls won't feel more than men feel," Mr. Jaffer says. "In circumcision, the feeling thing is cut."

Mr. Jaffer has already had his toddler girls circumcised. "We know that it hurts," he says, "but it is a must."

▪ Forever changed

Agnes Manyara says genital mutilation devastated her sex life. The wounds reopened the first few times she and her husband, Christopher, attempted intercourse. The weekend visits she had eagerly awaited quickly became ordeals.

"Our relations were painful," she says. "Sometimes I bled."

Still she was lucky that she suffered no long-term medical complications related to her attack.

At her parents' insistence, Mr. Manyara moved his wife and children from Munithu to a farm outside of Meru.

Nearly five hours by car from Nairobi, the tranquil town faces the southern side of Mount Kenya. Dense forests, family towns and vast tea and coffee plantations cover the steep hills that surround this county seat. The scent of coffee and bougainvillea blossoms blend in the crisp mountain air. Stacked burlap bags filled with coffee beans and tea leaves sit outside warehouses that line Meru's two paved roads.

"People here are friendly. I like it," says Mrs. Manyara.

Time and distance haven't diminished Mr. Manyara's anger.

"My mother never offered apologies" to Agnes, says Mr. Manyara, shaking his head. "I know in her heart she believes what she

230

did was proper. They wanted to make her like one of them."

Today, he says, his wife is quieter, less sure of herself and not nearly as friendly as she was when the couple met in 1978. Of course, he adds, their sex life isn't as pleasurable as it once was.

"What I'm trying to do, as much as possible, is to forget about what happened," Mr. Manyara says. "The elders feel that since nobody died, we should forgive these people. It is very difficult."

Mrs. Manyara seems more resigned to her situation.

"It is best that we live alone," she says, wiping away a bead of sweat that rolls down her forehead.

Late last year, at a family wedding, Mrs. Manyara saw her mother-in-law for the first time since the attack.

"She asked me to come back and live there.

"I said no."

April 18, 1993

This article appeared as part of The Dallas Morning News series, "Violence Against Women: A Question of Human Rights," which was awarded the Pulitzer Prize for international reporting on April 12, 1994.